"Whatever your walk of life, the ability to influence other people lies at the heart of success. This book takes you on a journey to become a strong influencer – whether you're influencing other people in the classroom, the boardroom or in your own home!"

BRIGADIER GARETH COLLETT CBE
Managing Director, Optima UK

"The Influence Book *cleverly brings to life the power of storytelling to win other people's hearts and minds. Nicole's step-by-step approach gives the reader the framework and confidence they need to build an engaging and influential story that delivers real results.*"

MEGHAN FARREN
Chief Marketing Officer KFC UK & Ireland, Yum Brands

"The *go-to-book for anyone who wants to inspire and motivate their team to raise up from their comfort zone, embrace change and reach their peak performance.*"

ANDY RIDDLE
Sales Director, KP Snacks

Published by
LID Publishing
An imprint of LID Business Media Ltd.
LABS House, 15-19 Bloomsbury Way,
London, WC1A 2TH, UK

info@lidpublishing.com
www.lidpublishing.com

A member of:

BPR⊛

businesspublishersroundtable.com

Printed by Severn, Gloucester

ISBN: 978-1-911687-98-6
ISBN: 978-1-915951-09-0 (ebook)

Cover and page design: Matthew Renaudin and Caroline Li

PRAISE FOR
THE INFLUENCE BOOK

"Nicole Soames is proving to be as dynamic in print as she is in the classroom. If you're looking to find that extra yard in life, The Influence Book is time extremely well invested."

OLLY DALE

Commercial Director, Liverpool Football Club

"A great read and a ton of practical takeaways. This book shows the real power of harnessing your EQ to listen with empathy, put yourself in the other person's shoes and build effective rapport. Soames shows convincingly how you can motivate people to establish a shared point of view and achieve so much more."

DR MARTYN NEWMAN

Clinical Psychologist specializing in Emotional Intelligence and Mindfulness, Author of *The Mindfulness Book*

"A must read – packed with expert advice, real life examples and easy-to-use exercises to help develop a confident mindset to take your influencing skills to the next level and improve your own performance."

DAMIAN MULCOCK

Vice President and General Manager, Cisco

THE INFLUENCE BOOK

**PRACTICAL STEPS
TO BECOMING A STRONG INFLUENCER**

NICOLE SOAMES

MADRID | MEXICO CITY | LONDON
BUENOS AIRES | BOGOTA | SHANGHAI

FOR OTHER TITLES
IN THE SERIES...

CONCISE ADVICE LAB

SMALL BOOKS: BIG IDEAS

CONTENTS

INTRODUCTION

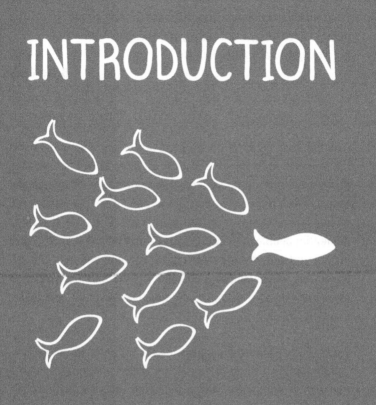

WHY
INFLUENCING
MATTERS

"Your ability to communicate, influence and persuade others to do things is absolutely indispensable to everything you accomplish in life."

Brian Tracy

As a business skills trainer and coach, I've come to understand the powerful role influence plays in all aspects of life. From the moment we are born, we learn the importance of influencing others to help us achieve our goals, whether it's in the playground, on the sports field or in the workplace. Consider the most influential people in the world today – they all share an ability to inspire and motivate others to take action and embrace change. By viewing influencing as a core life skill that can be developed over time, you too can build a powerful personal brand that leaves a lasting legacy.

Whether it's pitching a business idea to potential investors, persuading a client to agree to your proposal or cajoling kids into doing their homework, we all influence others every day. Yet, more often than not, we don't even realize we're doing it. We overlook these interactions and tend to see them as a type of selling, which, rightly or wrongly, has negative connotations for many. Selling is seen as pushy, aggressive or even manipulative behaviour. This can cause people to shy away from being front-footed, confident and in asking (influencing) mode. However, as behavioural science author Daniel Pink said in his book *To Sell Is Human*, "Like it or not we're all in sales now. Just because you don't have 'sales' in your job title doesn't mean you don't have to sell to people."

Whatever your walk of life, you invariably influence on a daily basis and you draw on your influencing skills to get people to agree to your point of view. Imagine a teacher who is an expert in their subject but fails to inspire and influence their students, or a website developer who creates technically brilliant new designs but doesn't have the communication and influencing skills necessary to persuade their client to implement the changes.

It's clearly time to change our mindset and view selling as a communication tool that **influences** others. Only then will you truly understand the immense value influencing can bring to your life, and make an effort to strengthen your daily influential interactions. This is particularly important in today's digital age, where we're bombarded with more information than ever before – much to the detriment of human interaction. Given this information overload, the ability to communicate personalized and meaningful messages is crucial to differentiating yourself and increasing your level of influence. So, whenever possible, resist the temptation to send an email or text to ask someone to help you and remember to ask them in person instead. This way you are far more likely to achieve your desired result. I'm a big believer that *people buy people*, so make it your priority to develop your emotional intelligence – those so-called soft skills that are often the most difficult to master – to help you win the other person's heart and mind.

1. WHAT EXACTLY IS INFLUENCING?
My career began in sales before I changed direction and became CEO of a leading business skills training and coaching company where we help people become strong influencers.

First things first – it's important to define exactly what we mean by influencing. My definition of influencing is: *"**The ability to leverage your emotional intelligence to communicate effectively so that you make it easy for the other person to say yes.**"*

In other words, strong influencers persuade others to come around to their way of thinking by building value in the person's mind and motivating them on an emotional level. *People buy people*, and the underlying premise at the heart of influencing is being 'liked'. This may sound like a cliché, but it's a cliché because it's true. It's easier to buy from someone you like and trust. As the author and motivational speaker Zig Ziglar said, "If people like you they'll listen to you, but if they trust you they'll do business with you." So, to achieve influencing success you should focus on the other person's needs – think about what's in it for them and why they should agree with you.

Some people mistakenly see influencing as a way of manipulating the other party to get their own way. In my experience this is true, in that most people like to be led so long as their needs have been taken into consideration. Take a moment to think about who has influenced you over your lifetime, both positively and negatively. It could be a teacher from school, a friend or a boss who influenced you and enriched your life in some way. On the other hand, you may have been pressured by someone into making a decision that left a bitter taste in your mouth. Use these experiences to consider what influencing best practice should look like. Remind yourself that when you're asked to do something by someone who influences you in a mindful way, you are more likely to do it, whereas if someone is demanding and doesn't take your needs into account you're more likely to resist, resent their request, or do it grudgingly. As we learn and appreciate the importance of emotional intelligence when persuading others, we understand that the ability to create a balanced relationship lies at the very heart of influencing. More about this in Part Three.

2. WHEN SHOULD YOU INFLUENCE?

Now that we have a clear picture of what it means to influence others, it's time to look at *when* we should do so. The three circles of influence shown in the diagram below explain when influencing skills should be used.

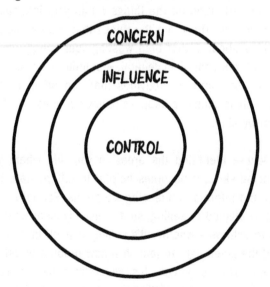

3 Circles of Influence
Adapted From Stephen Covey's book
Seven Habits of Highly Effective People (1989)

The inner circle represents the things that are completely within our control, such as where we live, the work we do, our attitude towards life, what we read and the words we use. **The middle circle** is our area of influence – those things that we can still do something about, such as the quality of our work, the relationships we form and the results we can achieve. **The outer circle** is our area of concern, touching on things over which we have no control – traffic, terrorism, foreign policy, the weather or natural disasters – that we can agonize over but ultimately are powerless to change.

The secret to becoming a strong influencer is to consciously focus your attention on the things within your influence circle (the inner ring). These are the things that you can actually do something about, rather than wasting your energy on matters outside of your control. In general, your influence circle includes short- to medium-term activities that can affect longer-term goals, such as changing people's behaviour or establishing new ways of working.

Once you've identified the areas in your life where you use influencing skills, it becomes helpful to differentiate between formal and informal influencing situations. Formal influencing is closely aligned to selling, so it is usually clear what you are trying to achieve – whether it's selling yourself in an interview, getting the green light to launch a new product or asking your boss for extra resources. It's generally easier to recognize influencing in a formal setting than in an informal one. This is because we're used to influencing customers, whereas we often fail to appreciate the importance and relevance of influencing other stakeholders.

The reality is that we're actually *informally* influencing others each and every day. It's happening whenever we try to get people aligned to our point of view. This could be persuading a friend to go to the cinema with you, discussing politics over a drink at the pub or asking someone on your team to work late.

The following exercise provides a great way to recognize just how prevalent informal influencing situations are.

EXERCISE
During the coming week, make note of every time you have to convince people to agree with your point of view. Remember, don't limit yourself to workplace scenarios – include examples where you've asked family or friends to agree with your ideas and arguments. You'll be amazed at how much influencing you're actually engaged in.

3. HOW EMOTIONAL INTELLIGENCE CAN HELP YOU INFLUENCE

If we refer back to our definition of influencing – *'The ability to leverage your emotional intelligence to help you communicate effectively so that you make it easy for the other person to say yes'* – there can be no doubt that developing your emotional intelligence is central to becoming a strong influencer.

One of the most influential people in my life has been clinical psychologist and emotional intelligence expert Dr Martyn Newman, who describes emotional intelligence as, *"A set of emotional and social skills that are most effective at influencing others."* It was through meeting Martyn and being trained as an emotional intelligence practitioner that I experienced my eureka moment. It was the realization that if I combined emotional intelligence with business skills training, I could make a seismic difference in people's performance and across all the relationships in their life.

The following diagram illustrates the four building blocks that make up emotional intelligence:

Strong influencers are able to draw on these core skills (Self-Management, Ambition, Social Skills and Self-Awareness) to build credentials and influence others. At the most basic level, developing your emotional intelligence makes it easy for the other person to say yes. To get there, you need to:

- Become aware of yourself and others.
- Have the necessary social and communication skills to build relationships.
- Control and manage yourself throughout the influencing conversation.
- Set the appropriate levels of ambition and optimism for the influencing situation you are in.

A good example of the role emotional intelligence plays in influencing would be a manager trying to motivate their team. In such scenarios, managers need to draw on their:

- Social skills – in particular their empathy – to understand the specific needs of each team member.
- Self-awareness to recognize how their management communication style impacts others.
- Self-control and self-confidence to establish credibility.
- Ambition to challenge team members to reach new heights.

4. YOUR JOURNEY TO BECOMING A STRONG INFLUENCER

Congratulations – just by starting this book, you're taking the first, very important step on your journey to becoming a strong influencer. Changing behaviour doesn't happen overnight – it takes ambition and hard work to develop your influencing skills. And all too often, we're so busy focusing on our 'day job' that we put our personal development on the back burner instead of taking steps to raise our game.

The Influence Book will provide a practical, accessible way to kick-start your efforts to become a better influencer. In my experience, most of the books on sales and influencing focus on the psychological aspect of selling. Instead, the aim of this book is to give you the tools and techniques necessary to apply influencing in everyday settings. I have deliberately made the difficult simple by breaking down the theory into manageable parts. As the saying goes, "How do you eat an elephant? In bite-sized chunks!" As you continue reading this book, you'll learn how to set yourself up for success, understand the importance of relationships, leverage the power of storytelling, and manage and control the influencing conversation so you can become a strong influencer in every aspect of your life.

By applying the tools and techniques detailed here, you will recognize that the secret to successful influencing is harnessing your emotional intelligence and taking the time to put your influencing skills into practice. The more hours you put in, the better influencing outcomes you will achieve and the more confident and assured you'll become. By putting emotional intelligence at the forefront of your daily life and creating this virtuous circle, you will reap the rewards of deeper and more meaningful relationships and improved performance. This is all within your reach, but you need to put in the time and effort.

PART ONE

DEVELOPING
A CONFIDENT
MINDSET

YOU CAN TEACH AN OLD DOG NEW TRICKS

As mentioned in the introduction, the first step to becoming a strong influencer is to change your mindset and see influencing as a life skill that can be developed over time. The secret to achieving this is to learn how to shift to a growth mindset – the deeply held conviction that you can be good at anything if you practice. Professor Carol Dweck, who first coined the term in her book, *Mindset: The New Psychology of Success*[1], argues that the power of believing that you can improve is the key to greater success in life. This is without question the case when it comes to developing your influencing skills.

Children are particularly open to learning new things, whether it's a musical instrument, a foreign language or a sport. Unfortunately, the older we get, the more fixed our mindset becomes, and we begin to underestimate the value of trying new things.

This can be attributed to complacency – *"I've been in sales for more than 15 years; what else do I need to know?"* Or, it could reflect an underlying fear of change – *"It's too late in my career to start learning new tools and techniques."* In either case, it can mean that you put your self-development on hold and focus on managing the daily grind of the here and now. However, given today's rapid pace of change, it's more important than ever to keep your skills up-to-date. And just as a world-class athlete continually strives to achieve the extraordinary, you need to keep raising the bar by following the steps on the subsequent pages to hone your influencing skills.

1. THE POWER OF SELF-KNOWLEDGE AND EMOTIONAL INTELLIGENCE

SOCIAL SKILLS

Relationship Skills
Empathy

SELF-AWARENESS

Self-Knowing
Straightforwardness

EMOTIONAL INTELLIGENCE

SELF-MANAGEMENT

Self-Control
Self-Confidence
Self-Reliance

AMBITION

Self-Actualization
Optimism
Adaptability

Self-knowledge is often described as the cornerstone of emotional intelligence. This is because self-improvement is virtually impossible unless you know exactly what makes you tick. So, your first task is to give yourself an open and honest appraisal. Try to be as objective as possible and write down a list of your key skills and strengths, and how they help you influence others. Examples of skills could be: strong persuasiveness, high levels of creativity, deep empathy, etc. Next comes the tricky part: identifying gaps, weaknesses and areas that need development. It's important that you find the courage to face your fears and acknowledge your Achilles' heel – perhaps you're secretly terrified of speaking in public or worry that you lack the communication skills necessary to effectively argue your point of view.

It's only by looking in the mirror and building a clear picture of the real you that you can hope to take the positive steps required to improve your influencing ability. Remember to ask for feedback from friends, family, customers or colleagues to help you identify any blind spots. This could be your customer reporting back that you're great at building rapport but lack attention to detail when it comes to discussing the numbers. By gathering information in this way, you will gain deeper insight into your influencing ability and the areas that need development.

A great tool to help you improve your self-awareness and personal development is the Johari Window, a technique developed by psychologists in the 1950s to help people better understand their relationships. It is illustrated on the next page.

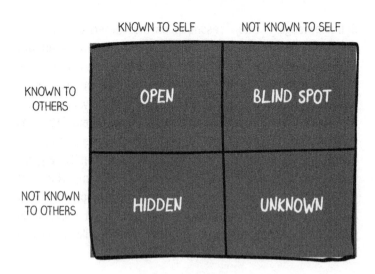

KNOWN TO SELF   NOT KNOWN TO SELF

KNOWN TO
OTHERS

NOT KNOWN
TO OTHERS

The Johari Window
(Luft and Harrington, 1955)

The OPEN box shows what is known to others and known to yourself. This could be that your communication style is gregarious and outgoing.

The HIDDEN box shows what is known to you but not known to others. These could be your personal fears or worries that you like to keep private.

The BLIND SPOT is what is known to others but not known to you. You may not even realize that you behave in a certain way. Perhaps you think that you are open to new ideas, when in fact you're often resistant to change.

The UNKNOWN window is what is not known to yourself or to others.

EXERCISE

Fill in the Johari Window below and start to develop your self-knowledge. Jot down those things that are known to you and others in the OPEN box, and what is known to you but unknown to others in the HIDDEN window. Then, take a guess at what could go in your BLIND SPOT box before testing these out with a coach or trusted advisor. By building your self-knowledge associated with the other three windows, you will automatically reduce the size of the UNKOWN window.

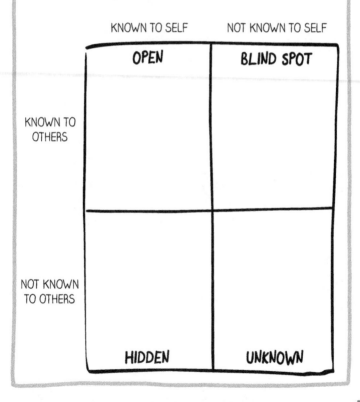

You will find that the greater your self-knowledge, the more comfortable you will be in your own skin and the better you'll become at influencing others. By understanding yourself and how *you* respond to various influencing situations, you will be better able to judge the reaction of others. Having the ability to recognize your own feelings lies at the heart of becoming a strong influencer. To do so you need to have a firm grasp of how you feel about the product or service you're offering, together with a clear understanding of what's motivating you, so that you can use all the skills at your disposal to successfully influence the other party.

EXERCISE

Fill in the table below to help uncover the motivation behind each influencing situation and how this makes you feel on an emotional level.

INFLUENCING SITUATION	MY MOTIVATION	HOW THIS MAKES ME FEEL
Meeting with a customer to sell a new product.	To meet my quarterly quota.	Worried I won't perform to the best of my ability and will let my team down.

By understanding what motivates you to influence a particular situation, you will be in a stronger position to prepare for influencing opportunities. In turn, these will boost your confidence so that you have a greater chance of achieving the outcome you desire through the power of influence.

2. UNLOCKING YOUR INNER CONFIDENCE

Having recognized where your strengths lie when influencing, and the areas that need development, now it's time to use this knowledge to boost your self-belief and challenge the status quo.

Strong influencers are action-orientated – they have the confidence to assert themselves and champion their ideas to make change happen. By setting new and ambitious goals for the future, you will harness your ambition – another key emotional intelligence skill – and reap the rewards of increased confidence and improved performance. After all, as the saying goes, "What doesn't challenge you doesn't change you." Carol Dweck reminds us of the importance of embracing change when she says, *"In a growth mindset, challenges are exciting rather than threatening. So rather than thinking, oh I am going to reveal my weakness, you say, wow, here's a chance to grow."*

A powerful tool that helps to set new influencing goals is the 3 Circles of Influence diagram we discussed earlier. It reminds us that our mindset resides within the inner circle of control and can be used to influence others.

EXERCISE

Think about your **circle of influence** and make a list of the areas in your life you'd most like to influence. Remember to differentiate between those factors that you can do something about and those that should be put in the circle of concern (over which you can have no control).

Next, proactively set yourself three goals for the year ahead. These could include improving your relationship with a customer, mentoring a new employee or becoming a thought leader in your field.

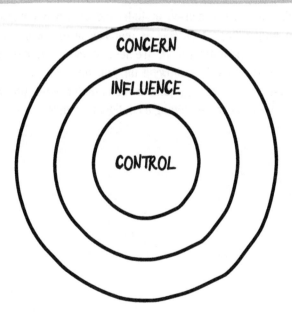

3 Circles of Influence

It's important to bear in mind that the goals within your influencing circle are more likely to be medium- to long-term, as they usually involve changing your or other people's behaviours, and this takes time. Don't expect to see immediate results. Perseverance and tenacity need to become your new best friends, and this means adopting that positive, confident *growth* mindset.

Strong influencers are almost always optimists at heart – they see things as changeable, cursory and circumstantial and believe they can make a difference. Pessimists, on the other hand, view things as personal, permanent and pervasive and often question whether it's even worthwhile trying to influence others. The secret to unlocking your inner confidence is to surround yourself with people who have a can-do attitude and banish any naysayers. When Jurgen Klopp took over as manager of the UK's Liverpool football club, he notably said, *"We need to change from doubters to believers – now."* By drawing on your optimism and viewing setbacks as learning opportunities rather than failures, you will be well on your way to developing a confident mindset.

3. BEING AUTHENTICALLY YOU

By accepting that you are not the finished article but a work in progress, you can use the knowledge you've uncovered about yourself to help convey *the real you* when influencing others. This means being authentic in your words, body language and tone of voice. This takes courage – it can be tempting to conceal any areas that need development with bravado. Some people mistakenly believe they need to 'fake it until they make it' in order to convince others of their expertise, but this rarely works. It is likely that everyone has at some point experienced someone trying to sell something using an over-rehearsed sales pitch. Nine times out of ten, you will find it cheesy or insincere and are likely to take your business elsewhere.

Strong influencers understand that the best communicators are able to connect with others in a genuine way. They recognize that being authentic helps to establish integrity and credibility – both of which are key influencing traits – since being authentic implies that you have nothing to hide. By being true to yourself and not just 'talking the talk', you'll build trust with the other party, making it easier for them to agree with your point of view.

Being a strong influencer also demands embracing imperfections. After all, no one is perfect and it's important to not pretend to be. Don't try to please people. Instead, be confident in your influencing ability and be prepared to show your vulnerability. This will show that you're approachable and help you to build a rapport with the other person. As Judy Garland said, "Always be a first-rate version of yourself and not a second-rate version of someone else."

A great way to understand how to become more authentic is to identify the influencing situations where you feel most comfortable. Do you feel at ease when you're influencing at home or are you in your element when you influence in the workplace? Try to capture this influencing confidence and transfer it to all elements of your life.

The key to authenticity is consistency. You need to make sure your personal brand – what Amazon CEO Jeff Bezos defines as, *"What people say about you when you're not in the room"* – is reflected in all the elements of your life. This may be sharing your opinion on LinkedIn or Twitter, your photos on Facebook or through your interactions with colleagues, customers, family and friends. Remember, people are prone to making snap judgements, so take steps to proactively manage your personal brand. By communicating in a consistent way, you'll develop an authentic voice that will boost your self-confidence and increase your credibility as a person of influence.

4. PEOPLE BUY PEOPLE

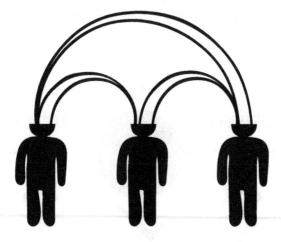

The majority of people like to do business with those they like. So, when influencing others, it's crucial to strike the right balance in appearing confident, in a way that falls somewhere between arrogance and subservience. In my experience, people in service-orientated industries tend to adopt a more subservient manner, whereas internal departments such as Sales, Marketing and Communications are more likely to take a more arrogant approach with one another. In either scenario, this will ultimately undermine your ability to influence the other party.

To understand why this is, consider how you feel when someone is subservient to you. Most would feel sorry for the deferential person or secretly want to take advantage of them. On the other hand, when someone comes across as arrogant, most people's natural instinct is to take them down a peg or two, or find a way to avoid them entirely.

Strong influencers effectively draw on their self-awareness and self-control so they can be appropriately confident. And this confidence is contagious – you need to believe in your own ability to make change happen in order to win other people's hearts and minds.

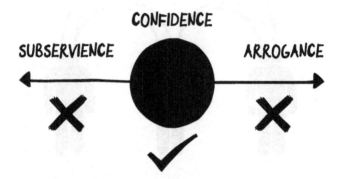

Finally, it's important to remember that developing a confident mindset doesn't happen overnight – it takes hard work and commitment. Take a look at the diagram opposite – it represents the learning pathway and shows the correlation between our level of competence and consciousness as we're trained in new skills.

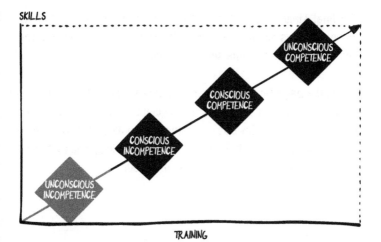

SKILLS

UNCONSCIOUS
COMPETENCE

CONSCIOUS
COMPETENCE

CONSCIOUS
INCOMPETENCE

UNCONSCIOUS
INCOMPETENCE

TRAINING

This pathway can be utilized as we become stronger at influencing. The majority of people will start the journey in the grey box, unaware of the knowledge required to become a strong influencer. In other words, you will be **unconsciously incompetent** – in a state of blissful ignorance!

As you progress through this book, you will undoubtedly begin to identify the gaps in your knowledge and specific areas of development required for advancement to the **consciously incompetent** stage. This may feel like a real stretch at first, and not entirely comfortable, especially if you've always considered yourself skilful at influencing. But to become stronger, you need to continue your learning journey and apply these skills more consciously, more frequently and in more situations so that you become **consciously competent**. This takes real thought, courage and effort.

The final stage of your learning pathway is unconscious competence, which is when your influencing skills are so practiced and refined they have become second nature.

This is the beginning of the learning pathway and will start the process of moving you out of the unconscious incompetence box. As you read the rest of this book, take the time to plot where you are on the learning journey to help track your progress, keep you motivated and inspire you to become a strong influencer.

KEY TAKEAWAYS

Here is a quick reminder of how to build a confident mindset:

- Adopt a growth mindset and recognize that influencing is a life skill that can be learned and developed over time.
- Draw on your self-knowledge to identify your influencing skills.
- Ask stakeholders for feedback in order to build a clear picture of *the real you* and take proactive steps to develop your influencing ability.
- Recognize your response to different influencing situations by understanding your underlying motivations and emotional needs.
- Harness your ambition to challenge the status quo and be an agent of change.
- Remember that what doesn't challenge you doesn't change you. Use the circles of control diagram to help set new influencing goals.
- Adopt a positive mindset. Remember that it takes time to achieve your influencing goals, so draw on your perseverance and resilience.
- Be authentic and connect with people in a genuine way.

PART TWO

SETTING
YOURSELF
UP FOR
INFLUENCING
SUCCESS

Now that you've got your head in the right space, it's time to focus on the steps required to set yourself up for influencing success. First off, you need to have a clear idea of what you want to achieve. This may sound obvious, but you'd be amazed how many people struggle to articulate exactly what they want to ask someone to say 'yes' to. So, it's hardly surprising that they find it difficult to win over the other person. After all, how can you possibly be sure-footed if you don't know where you're going?

Another reason a lot of people find themselves shying away is that they're worried about 'telling' others what to do. I always remind people that 'telling is the lowest form of selling' because it fails to take into account the other person's needs. Many of you probably know how it feels to be on the receiving end of an auto-mated payment protection insurance (PPI) call telling you why you need to make a claim. People often unwittingly tell, rather than sell, when they're too focused on what they want to get out of the conversation.

A secret to true influencing success is to create a need for the other party by asking yourself from the onset, "What's in it for them?" By using emotional intelligence to put yourself in the other person's shoes and identifying how to motivate them on an emo-tional level, you're laying the foundations for a strong influencing conversation. Sometimes you may already know their needs, in which case you'll need to confirm that this is so and show them how you can help them.

This Part will provide the tools and techniques necessary to pre-pare effectively for every influencing situation. The more thorough the preparation, the less daunting the influencing opportunity will become. By taking the time to do the homework, identifying what you want to achieve, and recognizing and responding to people's different communication styles, you'll reap the rewards of increased confidence, which will help you behave more authentically during the influencing conversation itself.

1. STARTING WITH THE END IN MIND

As noted, in order to be truly compelling when you influence you need to be really clear about what you want the other person to say 'yes' to. During workshops, I find that people generally have a vague idea of what they are asking for but lack the underlying details. As a consequence, they start to waffle when they open the influencing conversation or are weak in their call to action. Perhaps they have rushed their preparation or don't have the confidence to explain exactly what they're asking for. These are big beginner mistakes and explain why so many people take more time to influence than they actually need to.

The key to better influencing success is to prepare ahead. As Abraham Lincoln said, *"Give me six hours to chop down a tree and I will spend the first four sharpening the axe."* So, prior to your meeting, take the time to work out exactly what you are going to ask for. Remind yourself that, before you leave the room, the other party has to say yes to all of the elements you 'ask' for or recommend – not just the top-line concept. For example, if you want to ask for extra budget for your department, you need to spell out exactly how much you want, when it is required and what you're planning to spend it on.

Providing the whole picture means that there will be no surprises for either party. Remember: knowledge is power, and by being fore-warned both parties will be forearmed. The clearer you are in the call to action – using the full-picture method – the more confident you will feel and the more success you'll have. By preparing thor-oughly and seeing things from the other person's point of view, you will be able to answer any questions with confidence and head-off their concerns, saving precious time in the long run.

2. RECOGNIZING DIFFERENT COMMUNICATION STYLES

The second step in your preparation is harnessing your emotional intelligence so you can recognize different communication styles and the effect this will have on your conversation. It's useful to recall my definition of influencing: "The ability to leverage your emotional intelligence to **communicate** effectively so that you make it easy for the other person to say yes." Communication lies at the heart of what it means to be a strong influencer. Nonetheless, the majority of people underestimate the importance of understanding different communication styles when setting themselves up for influencing success.

Some people believe that they're not born as natural communicators. However, the great news for all of us is that communication skills, just like any other skills, can be honed and developed. The first step is to follow the fifth habit outlined in educator and author Stephen Covey's seminal book, *The Seven Habits of Highly Effective People*. Namely, "Seek first to understand, then to be understood." This is easier said than done because we're often more focused on getting our own point across and don't take the time to listen and understand the other person's point of view. The secret is to draw on your empathy – what clinical psychologist Dr Martyn Newman describes as 'the emotional glue of influence'[2] – to see things from the other person's perspective and uncover their true motivation.

As mentioned, people like doing business with people they like. So, it's important to be able to make a connection with stakeholders if you want to influence them. A powerful technique to help you find common ground is to communicate with others in a way that works for them, and the fastest route to achieving this is to understand *their* communication preferences.

There are lots of tools that can help you do this, and in my experience the easiest model to use is DISC, first outlined by the psychologist Dr William Marston in his book, *Emotions of Normal People.* The DISC model (shown below) breaks down communication into four different styles: Dominant & Driven; Influencing & Persuading; Security & Steady; and Compliant & Considered.

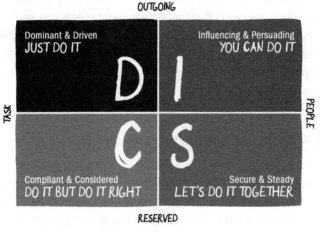

(Dr William Marston, 1929)

The DISC model is designed to help you recognize people's communication styles. On its own this is just data or insight, but by using your emotional intelligence and respecting others for their communication style – and responding appropriately – you will be able to build strong and meaningful relationships.

When you look at the diagram, it's important to remember that people are predictably different. All of us will fall somewhere along the axes of *outgoing to reserved* and *task orientated to people focus*. Outgoing types are fast-paced and get their energy from others, whereas reserved types are more measured and self-sufficient. People with a task preference will crave processes and plans, whereas those with a people preference will seek relationships and sharing. The DISC model will help you identify where you sit on these lines and assess the communication style of others.

Considering each communication style and its predominant characteristics helps in understanding and identifying each personality type. In the descriptions below each type is described in a slightly exaggerated way, so you can easily differentiate them. In reality, the differences between each style may be much less pronounced.

D STYLE - DOMINANT AND DRIVEN

Think of people who communicate in a demanding and direct manner. They're motivated by power and compelled to win and get results. As someone who is decisive and determined, their goal is to be in control and their most typical way to communicate is to tell others what to do.

You should be able to spot a **D** type person by their steady eye contact and straight talking. They are very businesslike and won't engage in chitchat – in fact, they're more likely to interrupt you as a way of exerting control. They are fueled by results, so the prospect of failing is a worry for them. As such, they dislike indecision and can be incredibly impatient. This makes them poor listeners – they believe it's their way or the highway and won't worry about upsetting someone's feelings.

I STYLE - INFLUENCING AND PERSUADING

These people are interactive and inspirational. They are motivated by praise and recognition. They're eager to get the job done, but unlike the hyper-focused **D**s they will want to have fun in the process. Their most likely communication style is to try and influence the other person.

An I type person wears their heart on their sleeve and will use expressive body language. They will be animated, enthusiastic and energizing. However, because they are people-orientated, want to be liked and crave recognition, they'll hold back on making unpopular decisions. They are big-picture people who shy away from complexity and, as a result, often lack attention to detail.

S STYLE - STEADY AND SECURE

These people are stable and supportive, and like to keep themselves on an even keel and make sure everyone is happy. Their preference is to organize everything, as they don't like conflict and want to preserve the status quo. As someone who always puts others first, their most likely communication style is to listen – they don't want to upset the apple cart with a disruptively strong opinion.

When you meet an **S** type of person you'll be struck by their friendly and sincere body language. They are easy-going and will ask lots of questions because they're genuinely interested in you. Always the diplomat, they avoid confrontation whenever possible and as a result don't like change or taking risks. They want to be accepted, so on occasion they can be overly sensitive or take things too personally. They also dislike being put under pressure.

C STYLE - COMPLIANT AND CONSIDERED

Picture people you know who are motivated by processes and procedures. They need to have a system in place and will be keen to point out what the rules are. Because they are conscientious and detailed, quality is very important to them. Their preference is to communicate in writing, as this allows them to take their time and be accurate and precise.

C types are the hardest to read because they don't show their feelings. They will be questioning, and want to understand all the details, so that they can use all the evidence available to them to make the right decision. They are perfectionists – they worry about being criticized and find it difficult to work with people who don't stick to the rules.

A great way to help you fully understand how this translates into different communication styles is to imagine being in an elevator with a group of people. **D** types will make a determined entrance, purposefully hitting the 'close the doors' button, while **I** types won't be able to resist making conversation with the other people. **S** types will be patiently holding the door open, saying there's plenty of room for more, and the **C** types will be calculating the weight of everyone in the elevator to make sure it doesn't exceed the maximum capacity!

By recognizing the other person's communication style – and they'll usually be a blend of these types – you will be more informed about how they make decisions, which will give you valuable clues as to the best way to influence them. So, from your first interaction with them, try to notice whether they are more outgoing or reserved. Was their first contact via email or did they pick up the phone to talk to you in person? It's generally easier to spot an outgoing person, so if you can't seem to read them the likelihood is that they are more private and therefore more reserved. See yourself as a detective, gathering evidence to test your thinking.

EXERCISE

Now it's time to test your ability to recognize different communication styles. Based on the DISC diagnostic model, match these famous faces with extreme versions of D, I, S and C.

D •	• Albert Einstein
I •	• Donald Trump
S •	• Richard Branson
C •	• Meghan Markle

My judgement says that Donald Trump is a **D** – you only have to watch his performance at a press conference to observe his dominant and demanding style. Richard Branson is clearly an **I** – an inspirational person who's built for fun. Megan Markle is a **S** – she is someone who cares deeply for others, as shown by her work for UNICEF and the way she interacts with crowds. Finally, Albert Einstein is a **C** – an analytical person with a research-based approach to life.

3. UNDERSTANDING YOUR OWN COMMUNICATION STYLE

By recognizing the four communication styles, you can gain a better understanding of your own style and the impact it has on others. So, take some time to self-reflect, or ask a trusted friend or coach for feedback to identify your communication style. This can be trickier than you think. People may have up to three different selves: the public self, the stressed self and the core self. Some people's communication style will be the same in all three scenarios, and what you see really is what you get. However, for others the three selves may be very different. Here's a quick overview of what you should look out for when you identify your own communication preferences.

1. **The Public Self** – This is the way you believe other people expect you to behave. It is the public image you'd like to present to the world and is therefore the most likely to change.
2. **The Stressed Self** – This is how you behave instinctively when you're feeling under pressure. When your adrenaline is pumping, the primal *flight or fight* instinct kicks in and will inevitably impact your communication style. This is the least likely to change.
3. **The Core Self** – This is the inner you. It is your private self and it should be where you feel most comfortable. This can change gradually over time.

A valuable method for differentiating between the three selves is to consider how you communicate on a good day versus a bad day. It can be difficult to admit to how you behave under pressure, especially if you don't necessarily behave well in such situations. However, it's important to remember that awareness is valuable and the better you know yourself the better you will become at influencing. So be open-minded, read the pros and cons of the different communication styles below, and see which resonate with you:

D STYLE - DOMINANT AND DRIVEN
On a good day you will be purposeful and productive but on a bad day you can be aggressive and controlling.

I STYLE - INFLUENCING AND PERSUADING
On a good day you will be enthusiastic and sociable but on a bad day you can be over-excitable and frantic.

S STYLE - STEADY AND SECURE
On a good day you will be caring and friendly but on a bad day you can be stubborn and resistant to change.

C STYLE - COMPLIANT AND CONSIDERED
On a good day you will be analytical and precise but on a bad day you can be suspicious and prickly.

Remember, you're likely to be a blend of two styles and might occasionally exhibit signs of three styles. Some people don't want to be a particular style. If you're that way, you need to draw on your emotional intelligence and have the self-confidence to accept who you really are. This is the only way to be truly authentic.

EXERCISE

Fill in the table below to help you clarify your particular communication style.

WHAT IS MY COMMUNICATION STYLE?	
HOW AM I ON A GOOD DAY?	
HOW AM I ON A BAD DAY?	

4. RESPONDING AND FLEXING YOUR COMMUNICATION STYLE

A benefit of understanding your own communication style is recognizing how this affects your relationships. For example, two **D** types could get on famously, as they have a similar outlook, or they could clash horribly since both are dominant and driven. A **C** type who is reserved and task-focused might feel intimidated by an outgoing, people-focused **I** type. Whatever the scenario, you'll be able to influence others far more convincingly if you respect their communication traits. Your focus should be on trying to align your styles to gain a clearer understanding of what motivates the other party, so you can build trust and respond to them accordingly.

HOW TO ALIGN YOUR COMMUNICATION STYLES

When you are influencing **D** types who make buying decisions based on quality and results, make sure you communicate in a concise way, backing up any statements with evidence. You need to stay focused – don't be tempted to go off on a tangent. **Watch out:** When two **D**s communicate, let the other person be in control or you will end up at loggerheads.

I types will make a spontaneous buying decision based on how your concept looks and feels. So, you need to flatter them, allow them to express themselves and help them turn this idea into reality. Remember to build in time for discussion so they can articulate their opinion. **Watch out:** When two **I** types communicate it is likely that they'll get on famously, but there's the risk of not making real progress since no one will focus on the details.

If you are influencing an **S**, recognize that they will only make a buying decision if they've had time to confer with others. They are more likely to say yes if your concept is simple and will be valued by others. So, you need to be patient and avoid putting them under pressure. Make sure you demonstrate that you've taken other people's points of view into consideration. **Watch out:** When two **S** types communicate, neither will want to put their heads above the parapet and make the difficult decision.

C types make methodical buying decisions based on warranties and comparisons. You therefore need to supply them with plenty of detail so they can consider each point. Be specific and give them the pros and cons so there are no surprises. **Watch out:** When two **C** types communicate, it will often be done by email and can become protracted and overly complicated.

Use the information above to help gather valuable clues, plot out the other individual's DISC profile and make note of what you should stop doing, what you should start doing and what you need to continue doing in order to influence them most effectively. Use the table below to help you plan for success.

THEIR NAME	STYLE ASSESSMENT	START	STOP	CONTINUE

Now that DISC is on your radar, use it whenever you want to influence someone. This can be done both formally and informally, and it really is where the magic happens. For example, if you're a manager you should be able to recognize the communication style of everyone on your team, so you can understand how best to motivate them to perform, deliver and raise their game. This could be through making quick decisions in your dealings with a D, praising an I for their hard work, taking the time to give a detailed brief to a C and remembering to show consideration for an S's point of view. By preparing ahead of time in this way, valuing people's differences and speaking a common language, you will immediately reap the rewards of improved relationships with others.

KEY TAKEAWAYS

We've covered a lot of ground in this Part, so here's a quick summary of the key steps you need to take to set yourself up for influencing success.

- Understand exactly what you want to achieve in the influencing conversation.
- Start with the end in mind – ask yourself what's in it for the other party.
- Use your emotional intelligence to put yourself in the other person's shoes, and by doing so determine how to motivate them to agree with your position.
- Plan for success – prepare thoroughly for each influencing situation.
- Use the DISC tool to determine the communication style of others in order to plan how best to influence them.
- Draw on your self-awareness to understand your own particular influencing style and how this will impact others.
- Ask yourself how you communicate on a bad day, and on a good day, so you understand how your own communication style can differ.

PART THREE

UNDERSTANDING THE IMPORTANCE OF RELATIONSHIPS

As you begin to recognize your communication style and that of others, you will communicate better and more authentically, and people will in turn like you better. This will result in stronger relationships because people like doing business with people they like. The better your relationship skills, the stronger you will become at influencing. This quickly becomes a virtuous circle, which reduces tension and conflict, making influencing seem natural and seamless.

Finding common ground also helps to build strong relationships by balancing the playing field, which helps forge real connections. To do this effectively, you need to understand the other person's needs and step into their shoes – only then will you be able to motivate them to say yes on a personal, emotional and commercial level. This is where your emotional intelligence comes to the forefront. By demonstrating that you see things from their perspective, you'll build a better relationship and make that shift from telling into selling. This will help ensure that the other person does not feel manipulated or out-manoeuvred during the influencing conversation.

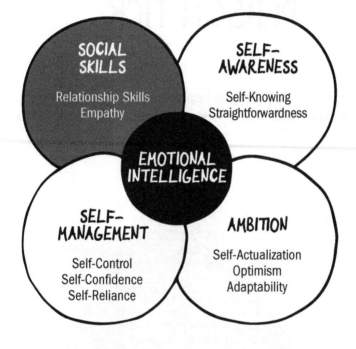

SOCIAL
SKILLS

Relationship Skills
Empathy

SELF-
AWARENESS

Self-Knowing
Straightforwardness

EMOTIONAL
INTELLIGENCE

SELF-
MANAGEMENT

Self-Control
Self-Confidence
Self-Reliance

AMBITION

Self-Actualization
Optimism
Adaptability

1. UNDERSTANDING WHAT MAKES THE OTHER PERSON TICK

A powerful tool that can help put you in other people's shoes is psychologist Abraham Maslow's Hierarchy of Needs theory. See below[3].

SELF-ACTUALIZATION
morality, creativity, spontaneity, acceptance

SELF-ESTEEM
confidence, achievement, respect of others

LOVE AND BELONGING
friendship, family, intimacy, sense of connection

SAFETY AND SECURITY
health, employment, property, family and social stability

PHYSIOLOGICAL NEEDS
oxygen, food, water, shelter, clothing, sleep

Abraham Maslow, *A Theory of Human Motivation* (1943)

Maslow suggested that there are five stages of human needs. He said people are motivated by certain needs that must be fulfilled in a specific order. The only way to reach your full potential, he asserted, is by satisfying each need in turn, starting from the lowest level (stage one) and progressing up through the highest level (stage five).

According to Maslow's hierarchy:

- The first stage comprises physiological needs – the essentials required for survival, such as water, food and air.
- The second stage is the need for safety, whether it's health or stability at home and at work.
- The third stage is the need to belong and includes our relationships with friends, family and colleagues.
- The fourth stage is our need for self-esteem and self-confidence.
- The fifth and final stage is self-actualization – it embodies our need for personal growth and self-development.

By applying this theory to those you're trying to influence, you can gain a clearer understanding of what will motivate them to say 'yes' to you. For example, imagine you're hiring a new employee and have shortlisted two people for the role. Candidate A has been made redundant in the past so needs job security and is therefore at stage two; candidate B has a lot of confidence and craves respect, so is at stage four. You will need to influence these individuals in different ways by putting yourself in their respective shoes. With the first candidate this could involve reassuring them that they will have a six-month notice period, and for the second candidate this could involve selling the high-profile nature of the role.

The ability to understand the needs of others is crucial to influencing success, and it takes skill and effort. You need to ask yourself:

- What are the particular challenges the other party is facing?
- What opportunities are there for them?
- How can you help them meet these needs or overcome their specific challenges?

HOW TO UNCOVER YOUR CUSTOMER'S NEEDS

Here, Maslow's hierarchy pyramid has been adapted to help uncover the needs of others in a more formal influencing situation.

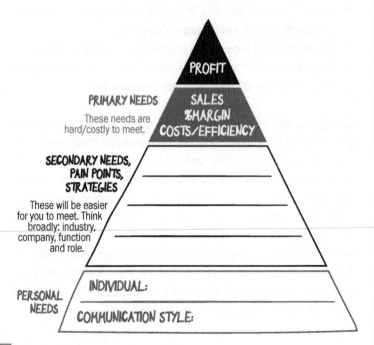

PROFIT

PRIMARY NEEDS
These needs are hard/costly to meet.

SALES
%MARGIN
COSTS/EFFICIENCY

SECONDARY NEEDS, PAIN POINTS, STRATEGIES
These will be easier for you to meet. Think broadly: industry, company, function and role.

PERSONAL NEEDS

INDIVIDUAL:

COMMUNICATION STYLE:

This diagram shows that the primary need of a business is to make a profit. This is achieved by selling products or services at a margin, by charging the right price and being cost efficient. These primary needs are the outcomes of delivering against secondary needs, which sit below. So by focusing on understanding the customer's secondary needs – their strategies and pain points – a business will increase the chances of being able to successfully influence them.

Take the time to fill out the pyramid for each of your customers or stakeholders. It's helpful to build up a wide range of secondary needs. For instance, consider how much time and effort they will put into the strategies that are working well, or the areas that need fixing.

Be sure to explore their industry, sector, company, function or role. If your customer is a soft drinks manufacturer, one of their pain points could be the introduction of new laws or regulations, such as a sugar tax. One of their strategies might be to reformulate their drinks in a way that doesn't adversely affect the taste but mitigates the impact of the new tax. On a personal level, they may be feeling stressed or overwhelmed by the amount of work ahead of them and worried about how to manage their team's morale. By considering all of these factors, you will understand their hierarchy of needs and be able to create an influencing story that shows how you can help them solve their problems or create new opportunities. Remember, their secondary needs will change over time, so best practice is to keep updating this triangle to factor in any new developments.

Once you have a clear idea of your customer's needs, check that your proposal actually meets some of them. Otherwise, you ought to examine why you're trying to influence them in the first place. Remember, if you don't take their needs into account, you are *telling* and not *selling*!

HOW TO CREATE NEEDS
FOR YOUR CUSTOMER

Beyond uncovering existing 'known' needs, strong influencers are able to create new needs in the minds of others. After all, we all have needs that we don't know we have. As Henry Ford famously said, *"If I had asked people what they wanted, they would have said faster horses."*

The most effective way of creating desire in people's minds is through the use of data and insights that demonstrate how you can help them improve. How open they are to being influenced in this way will depend on how they measure themselves. If they feel they're performing worse than expected, they are more likely to recognize the need for help. If their performance is in line with their expectations, they may or may not want your offer to help them do even better. If they believe they're performing at the top of their game and are excelling beyond their expectations, they are less likely to be open to your ideas and suggestions.

The key to creating a need is to make a comparison that resonates with someone by considering their particular mindset. The challenge is to choose the most relevant point of comparison for the individual in question. For example, some people measure their performance against their competitors, whereas others weigh it against a previous year's performance. The better their performance, the more creative you'll have to be in identifying a comparison that motivates them on an emotional or commercial level. Remember to choose the comparison that creates the biggest growth opportunity for them, and one that they'll recognize as stretching, opportunistic and in their line of sight. After all, you're trying to motivate them.

Once you have identified the relevant performance gap, you need to calculate the benefit you're prepared to deliver. For example, if their business is worth £10m annually and their growth of 10% has now stalled, you could calculate that their commercial gap is £1m. (When multiplying their turnover of £10m by 10% you arrive at the £1m opportunity gap.) The reason this comparison is so powerful is that they may not have focused on this metric or had time to review their performance in detail. By discussing their performance objectively and using your emotional intelligence to explain how you can help them improve, they're more likely to listen and embrace your ideas.

Don't worry if they don't completely agree with your numbers or comparison. Your overriding aim should be to create the appropriate context for your idea by demonstrating that you understand and genuinely care about their needs. Remember, you only have to outline one compelling opportunity to capture their attention. Don't be overwhelmed by the vast amount of information available online – be selective and choose the comparison you think will best resonate with them.

2. USING YOUR EMOTIONAL INTELLIGENCE TO ASK CLEVER QUESTIONS

Now that you've done your research and identified how your proposal will meet the person's secondary needs, you should consider the primary needs that will be impacted. Remember, you only want to discuss the needs you know you can help with – otherwise you risk frustrating them. So be focused and purposeful, draw on your emotional intelligence and use clever questions to gain greater clarity. For example, if you find that one of their needs is to be seen as more innovative in the marketplace, and your proposal is to help them launch an original new product, the question to ask could be, "How important is innovation to your growth agenda?" This question skilfully combines your technical knowledge (understanding of the market) with your emotional intelligence (understanding of the person) and your IQ (intelligence) to uncover a need that you know you're able to meet.

By using questions like this you can show genuine interest in the individual and their agenda. This line of inquiry is great for building rapport and establishing long-term relationships. Strong influencers do this by drawing on their empathy and using different types of questions to get people to open up.

The first step is to ask an open question, such as, "What are the most exciting elements of your strategy?" Or, "How does this impact your plans for next year?" These types of question will help you gather information because they require descriptive answers and encourage the other party to confide in you.

The second step is to ask a closed question, such as, "Is this still a top priority for you?" Or, "Are you planning to launch this product next year?" Closed questions drive a 'yes' or 'no' response and are useful for clarifying facts and confirming details of previously identified needs.

EXERCISE

Use the table below to help plan ahead by writing down the key needs your ideas can meet and the different types of questions you can ask to uncover them. By preparing ahead in this way, you'll find it easier to open up the conversation and listen attentively as the other party reveals their needs.

NEEDS MY PROPOSAL MEETS	CLEVER QUESTIONS TO UNCOVER THESE NEEDS

Whenever you ask your counterpart a question, it's important to bear in mind their particular communication style so you can adapt your approach accordingly. Let's have another look at the DISC chart to remind you of the different styles.

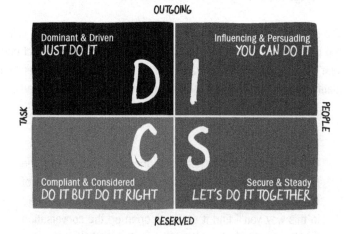

If, for example, you ask a **C** personality type endless questions, they may become suspicious and stop answering, whereas asking an **I** type lots of open questions may encourage them to go off on a tangent. So, use your knowledge of their communication style to choose the right language when probing them on their agenda.

WATCH OUT FOR THESE
ROOKIE MISTAKES:

- **Asking *"How's business?"***
  - » On the surface this question seems like a good one to ask, as it shows interest, but it's too vague and makes it difficult for someone to articulate a detailed response.
  - » It also infers that you don't know how they're performing – that you haven't invested the time to find out!
  - » Remember, if you ask a vague question you are more likely to get a vague answer!

- **Asking *"What are your top priorities?"***
  - » Although this is an open question, it's too high-level.
  - » The answer to this question is unlikely to provide a thorough understanding of the specific challenges or opportunities the other party is prioritizing.

- **Asking 'validation' questions**
  - » These are questions that will provide you with detailed information, such as finding out how much stock they've issued or what their budget is.
  - » The answer to such questions may be sensitive, so you need to use a 'clever' approach to open up a conversation where the other party is comfortable sharing their needs.
  - » Do not ask direct questions, as these could make the other person feel uncomfortable.

- **Not asking any questions at all**
  - » If you are too focused on your own agenda, or believe you already know what makes the other person tick, you could be tempted to forgo asking any questions whatsoever.
  - » Do this at your peril, as you are more likely to overlook or misunderstand their real needs or motivations.

3. LISTENING WITH EMPATHY

Almost all books about selling or influencing discuss the value of asking questions, but they rarely cover the importance of using emotional intelligence when listening to responses. This may sound obvious, but people generally underestimate the level of effort required to listen attentively to the other party. Remember, hearing is involuntary, whereas listening is a skill.

The first step in developing your listening skill is to suspend judgment and remember that you are not *waiting to talk*. You're there to listen to what the other individual has to say and uncover their needs.

There are three levels of listening, each encompassing different types of motivation, attention and focus. Becoming aware of them can help hone your listening skills. See the diagram opposite.

LEVELS OF LISTENING

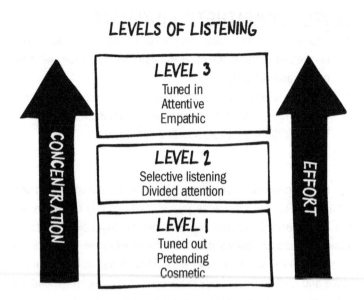

CONCENTRATION

LEVEL 3
Tuned in
Attentive
Empathic

LEVEL 2
Selective listening
Divided attention

LEVEL 1
Tuned out
Pretending
Cosmetic

EFFORT

LEVEL 1: COSMETIC LISTENING

- This involves pretending to hear what the other party is saying, but actually thinking about something else entirely.
- Perhaps you are too focused on what you want to say next, or maybe you don't have the capacity to listen properly because you're only interested in your own agenda.

LEVEL 2: SELECTIVE LISTENING

- We are all guilty at times of just hearing the things we want to hear.
- For example, you may only listen to the needs you have pre-pared for and ignore any information that contradicts it.
- Therefore, use your emotional intelligence to become more open-minded and adaptable, so you can take in the bigger picture.

LEVEL 3: EMPATHETIC LISTENING

- This level requires using emotional intelligence to listen and be present in the moment so you can process exactly what the other party is saying.
- It takes real effort and concentration and involves reading their body language and tone of voice, as well as the words they use, to gain a thorough understanding of their needs.

The best connections come from being able to use your emotional intelligence to listen, because your ultimate goal is to understand the other person's perspective. Research by psychology professor Albert Mehrabian[4] shows that only 7% of what we communicate comes from the words we use, while 38% comes from our tone of voice and 55% from our body language. So, it's crucial to 'read' the other person's interactive style to get the full picture.

4. BUILDING RAPPORT

By uncovering and creating needs, asking clever questions and listening with empathy, you will be well on your way to building rapport with the other person. First impressions really do count, so think of building rapport as a way of fast-tracking your relationship. Show genuine interest by being truly present in the moment and using commonalities to connect.

Make sure that the other party looks forward to seeing you again, since you're laying down the groundwork for your relationship going forward. In my experience, people often focus on building rapport in the early stages of their interactions but can quickly become lazy and take the relationship for granted. Below are some typical examples of how people inadvertently break rapport:

- Making assumptions.
- Getting too personal too soon.
- Being inflexible.
- Not preparing the next steps
- Adding opinion inappropriately.
- Being in a hurry.

Strong influencers, on the other hand, understand the need to nurture relationships by constantly making connections with the other person, regardless of how many times you've met them. The more effort you put in, the more you should expect back and the more equal your relationship will become. Refer back to the learning pathway – your aim should be to become unconsciously competent by building rapport so that it feels like second nature.

Ultimately, by building rapport you will establish trust, which is critical for building strong and meaningful relationships. The following equation demonstrates the important role it plays.

$$TRUST = \frac{RELIABILITY + CREDIBILITY + EMPATHY}{SELF-INTEREST}$$

The equation shows that trust can be built by delivering on your promises (reliability), having the relevant experience and expertise (credibility), and being able to put yourself in the other party's shoes (empathy), while minimizing your personal agenda (self-interest). If you're too focused on yourself, the level of trust will automatically go down and you'll be less likely to influence them to say 'yes'.

A final piece of advice for understanding relationships is to draw on your knowledge of communication styles, and to always be curious, interested and appropriately confident. Only then will you have the insight, rapport and trust you need to create an influencing story that wins other people's hearts and minds. We'll take a closer look at how to do this in the next Part.

KEY TAKEAWAYS

The focus of this Part has been on understanding of the steps required to build trust and rapport, and how to motivate others on a personal, emotional and commercial level.

Here's a quick recap of the main points:

- Draw on your knowledge of communication styles with emotional intelligence to see things from the other party's perspective.
- Use Maslow's Hierarchy of Needs to uncover the other party's needs and motivations.
- Analyze the other party's challenges and opportunities and consider how you can help them.
- Once you've uncovered these needs, confirm that your proposal fulfills at least some of them.
- Ask clever questions to help identify needs that you know you're able to satisfy.
- Use open and closed questions to connect and clarify both known and unknown needs.
- Build trust and rapport by being credible, reliable and empathetic.
- Always be curious, ask questions and be appropriately confident.
- Listen with empathy – real-time, in the moment – so that you can really think, feel and understand things from their perspective.

PART FOUR

INFLUENCING
THROUGH
STORY TELLING

The next step to becoming a strong influencer is using the insights gathered about the other person's needs and communication style to create a tailored story that makes it easy for them to say 'yes' to you. Even if you feel that creative writing is not your forte, it's worth pointing out that *everyone* can learn to tell a good story – it just takes practice.

In this Part, you will find easy-to-use tools and techniques that can help structure compelling, influential stories to show how you can help the other party meet their needs.

1. THE POWER OF STORYTELLING

"The most powerful person in the world is the storyteller. The storyteller sets the vision, values and agenda of a whole generation to come." These words by Apple founder Steve Jobs reflect how valuable storytelling can be in helping you make connections and influence other people. Throughout human history, as our languages developed, stories have been at the root of our ability to communicate and understand the world around us. Stories capture our attention and engage us on an emotional level in a way that facts and figures do not. Research[5] shows that we are 22 times more likely to remember a story than facts alone. It's not surprising that Rudyard Kipling remarked, *"If history were taught in the form of stories, it would never be forgotten."*

With this in mind, your goal should be to create an engaging, influential story that wins the other party's heart and mind. The more visual and connected you can make the story, the more powerful and effective it will be. There are essentially six storytelling techniques that will help to build a memorable picture and support your argument or explanation.

STORYTELLING TECHNIQUES

1. **Use analogies** – A great example of this is when Steve Jobs said, "A computer is the equivalent of a bicycle for our minds." The use of compelling parallels helps to connect people on an emotional level.

2. **Ask rhetorical questions** – An example would be, "Why is innovation important to business today?" These types of questions are useful tools that prompt the other party to think. They also enable you to introduce and communicate important messages.

3. **Use reiteration** – Repetition is an effective way to secure a key point. In his most famous speech, Winston Churchill showed the power of reiteration with, "We shall fight on the beaches. We shall fight on the landing grounds. We shall fight in the fields, and in the streets, we shall fight in the hills. We shall never surrender."

4. **Sell the numbers** – Always present numbers in the best way possible to support your argument. This could mean breaking down large numbers so they seem smaller or making small numbers seem larger. For example, offering a 90-day warranty, as opposed to 3 months, seems like a better offer.

5. **Paint a picture** – Add visuals to bring your story to life, but remember that they shouldn't replace key data or insight. For example, create mock-up imagery for the new product you're trying to sell, or draft an imagined press release to show the other party what success would look like.

6. **Refer to third parties** – Making comparisons to third parties is an effective way to introduce a different perspective and establish credibility.

2. PEOPLE BUY THE *WHY*, NOT THE *WHAT*

WHY?

As you put together your influential story, it may help to follow the advice given by organizational consultant Simon Sinek in his famous TED Talk, *How Great Leaders Inspire Action*.[6] According to Sinek, *"People don't buy what you do; they buy why you do it."* In explaining why we buy our computers from Apple, as opposed to their competitors, Sinek argues that it's because we buy into the company's belief that everything they do challenges the status quo.

Applying Sinek's theory of inspiring others through your influential story demands that you focus on **why** the other party should say 'yes' to your proposal, by demonstrating **how** you can help them close their performance gap, instead of telling them **what** you can offer them. This influencing approach flies in the face of the traditional methods that focused on communicating your unique selling point (the **what**), which can be an uphill battle. By leading with the **why** and applying Sinek's philosophy to the crux of your story, you're likely to engage better with the other person and show them **how** you can help satisfy their particular needs.

3. SELLING EVERY ASPECT OF YOUR PROPOSITION

This approach was briefly covered in Part Two, regarding starting out with the end in mind. However, since this is critical to the success of your influencing story it warrants further coverage here.

In order to build a compelling story, the other party should be influenced on **everything** you want them to agree to, not just your top-line proposition or recommendation. To succeed in this, all the reasons why they should say 'yes' to your recommendation must be made clear. Explain why each aspect is a good idea and prove why it will work, using data, insight or visuals. In other words, you need to sell the benefits of what you're offering instead of touting the features.

A great way to understand the difference between features and benefits is to imagine that you have to sell a felt-tip marker to a friend who typically buys a ballpoint pen, and whose child is about to start a new school. One of the features you have to sell is that it is a permanent marker. But this will only be of benefit if they have a need for this feature – and in this case, you know that your friend will *need* to label their child's new school uniform.

It is far more effective to sell the benefits than it is to list the features. So, a more persuasive way to sell the marker would be to say, "The ink never fades no matter how many times you wash the clothes." Or, "It takes a third of the time to write on the label than it would to stitch in a personalized woven label." This approach can be even more powerful when the benefits are backed up with evidence. In this example, you could quote the number of hours others have saved using the permanent marker compared to those who sewed a label on by hand. The more proof you can provide, the more objective your story will seem and the more likely the other person is to agree with your proposition – in this case, to agree to buy the marker.

By building your story in this way and relating it back to the other party's needs, you are likely to motivate them on both an emotional and commercial level. Remember, your aim should be to make the decision feel like a no-brainer. So, keep asking yourself the following questions:

- What's in it for them?
- How can I prove it?
- Why should they say yes?

4. MAKING IT EASY FOR THEM TO SAY YES

This is the final step in developing a compelling influencing story, and the point where everything should be pulled together. At this stage, the other party should be shown the size of the prize that will be delivered with this change. This means making robust assumptions about the benefit the other person will see if they adopt everything you've recommended, after deducting any investment required. The more relevant you can make this, the easier it will be for them to say 'yes'.

So, it is important to consider the language used and see things from their perspective. In the marker vs. ballpoint pen example, the marker will be more expensive than a ballpoint, so you'll need to effectively articulate how changing this buying behaviour will be of benefit and how the additional cost will be justified. To do so you could compare the price of the marker to the total cost of personalized woven labels, needles and cotton.

100 personalized labels cost £20
+ the needles £3.50 + cotton thread £1.50
= the total cost of £25

VS

The permanent marker costs **£5**

It is easier for the other party to say 'yes' to cost saving than to say 'yes' to paying more for a product that they wouldn't normally buy. So in this example, it is key to highlight the financial saving.

During influencing situations, many people are nervous about projecting the net benefit. Yet, if you don't do so you run risk of the other party doing it themselves, and less optimistically. Remember that it's a projection, not a promise, since it depends on how well the other party implements your suggestions, and that's ultimately out of your control. Instead, be confident that you've prepared your best view – after all, if you don't actually believe the numbers yourself, you'll struggle to convince the other party to believe them.

5. ADOPTING A DISCIPLINED APPROACH

When it comes to creating your influencing story, it's important to remember that less is more. So, spend the time and put the right story together. In formal influencing situations, people tend to spend hours pulling together a detailed presentation that's packed with information, a lot of which isn't relevant. Not only is this time-consuming, but it can also muddy the water for everyone involved. Instead of boring the other person with endless facts and showcasing your knowledge, make sure your message is concise and that there's little room for confusion. This will make it easier for the other person to say 'yes'.

As mentioned earlier, everyone can learn to be a good storyteller by following a framework that helps him or her review and deliver their story. Storyboarding is a powerful technique for preparing compelling, influential stories and can be used in a conversation or a more formal influencing presentation. It's a tried and tested technique used by advertising agencies, movie makers and authors to help visualize key points. It is a time-efficient and disciplined way to prepare, as it helps you to order your thoughts and identify exactly what you need to include so that your story makes a real impact.

Here we will use the **STRONG** influencing storyboard approach, which includes six main steps:

- First, **Set the scene** by creating the context for your story and setting up the needs of the person you're trying to influence.
- Then, **Tailor the story**, explaining why the person should say 'yes' to your recommendation and making sure you sell every aspect of the proposal.
- Next you summarize your **Recommendation**. You are in effect repeating a condensed form of the story – kind of like an executive summary.
- Finally, explain the **Opportunity** or the size of the prize. This is your 'what's in it for them' statement and is the part of the story they'll be most interested in.
- Now that you've walked through all of these steps, the time has come to **Negotiate**.
- Finally, with everything else sorted out, all that's left is to **Get on to next steps**.

Try to think of the STRONG framework as a way to order your thoughts – like an organized mind map.

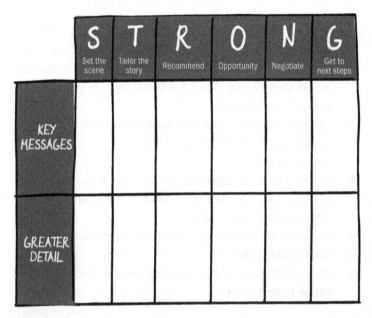

	S Set the scene	T Tailor the story	R Recommend	O Opportunity	N Negotiate	G Get to next steps
KEY MESSAGES						
GREATER DETAIL						

HOW TO FILL IN YOUR STRONG STORYBOARD

You always need to start with the recommendation (what's in it for them) and work backwards – Recommend, Tailor the Story, Set the Scene, Opportunity, Negotiate, Get to Next Steps (RTSONG). Initially, this may seem a bit confusing, so a step-by-step framework has been provided to guide you through the STRONG storyboarding in the most beneficial order.

You can map out your thoughts if you re-create a STRONG storyboard on a horizontally rotated piece of printer paper.

STAGE ONE:

Think big-picture first. Before you dive into the detail, take a step back and think about the key messages you want to land. Ask yourself what main themes of the story you really want them to remember.

Your first step is to fill in the key messages section of the storyboard; these will form the chapter headings of your story. I have added an example to help you bring the storyboarding technique to life – in this case the scenario is that you want to persuade your partner to upgrade your family car to a hybrid sport utility vehicle (SUV).

R – Start with your recommendation

- Write down your top-line proposal – the ambitious request that you want them to say 'yes' to. Then work backwards from here.

  Example: *We need to buy a new hybrid SUV before the summer holidays.*

T – Tailor the story

- Make a note of what will bring your proposition to life. Ask yourself what the key message is – as the centerpiece of the story – that supports your recommendation.

  Example: *Hybrids are good for the environment and are a cost-effective way to travel.*

S – Set the scene

- Identify the need and the macro opportunity that appropriately sets the scene in the other party's mind.

  Example: *The cost of flights and car rentals have risen by 15% in the past year so it will be cheaper to drive to your holiday destination.*

STAGE TWO:

Now zoom in from the big picture to the smaller picture. This is where you start to add detail to your presentation or conversation.

R – Go back to the Recommendation

- Write down your clear, specific request, and what it is worth to the other party commercially and emotionally, even if you have to work out the details later.
- Remember, your recommendation is the anchor of your story. Spend time getting this right because everything flows from here.
  Example: *We need a new hybrid SUV with free roof rack and bike box delivered, and installation of the electrical charging point in the house, before the 24th of July. This will provide us with a cost saving of £1,600.*

T – Tailor the story

- This is where you bring your idea to life.
- Write down the key headline that supports your proposition or recommendation.
- You need to sell the 'why' for every part of your recommendation.
- Remember to *talk features* and *sell benefits*.
- Note down – and potentially illustrate in presentation form – any data sources that can help give weight to your rationale.
  Example: *Hybrid SUVs are environmentally friendly and cut fuel costs in half. The new hybrid limited edition includes free bike rack and roof box and is available by mid-July. The installation of the charging point is hassle-free and one charge lasts for 500 miles.*

S – Set the Scene

- This is all about the other party – identify the needs that are answered by the key headlines in tailoring your story.

- Write down the macro trend/opportunity.
- Quantify the size of their prize – after all, influencing should commercially or emotionally motivate the other party.
- Prepare your clever questions to uncover the other person's needs.
  Example: *Purchasing the SUV will save £2,000 on the cost of the flights and car rental on the family holiday. It also offers a child-friendly travel option with no weight restrictions on luggage.*

O – Opportunity
- Show them the size of the opportunity in detail and how this benefits them in a relevant, practical way.
- Break it all down and if necessary draw a graph to illustrate it. Remember, a picture speaks a thousand words.
  Example: *The cost of flights and car rental is £2,000, the annual cost saving on fuel is £600, minus the additional monthly car payment of £1,000, yielding a total saving of £1,600.*

N – Negotiate
Negotiating is a completely different skill than influencing, which is why I've devoted an entire book to the subject. (See *The Negotiation Book*[7] for practical advice on how to become a master negotiator.) However, in the context of building your influencing story, it's vital to finish influencing before you start negotiating. And so, remember to:
- Try and anticipate any possible curveballs that may come your way.
- Create solutions to any real issues or challenges the other party may have with your idea. (More on how to do this in Part Six.)
- Prepare different variables to bring to the table and broaden the deal.

G – Get to next steps

- Identify what needs to happen, and by when.
- Prepare your follow-up actions and note them down.
- Outline different ways to keep the lines of communication open.
- If you're preparing a presentation to share with the other party, use your judgment in deciding whether to add this into the project plan or simply talk about it.

  Example: *Let's book the test drive for next week and agree on the colour.*

Once you have completed your storyboard, show it to someone else. It should be immediately obvious to them what you're talking about. Your headings should be your *elevator pitch* – short and sweet. This will help you recognize whether you story is a compelling one or not. It will take time and effort to pull together a storyboard for the first time, but the more you do it the easier it becomes. Here are some helpful tips for storyboarding:

- Try not to take longer than an hour to storyboard your initial thoughts.
- Scrutinize whether you're being ambitious enough in your call to action.
- Don't focus too much on what you want to get out of the conversation.
- Keep asking yourself 'so what?' from the other person's point of view.
- Share your storyboard with colleagues or your manager for feedback.

Finally, if you want to build trust with the other party you need to be authentic. So, resist the temptation to look at other people's presentations as templates for pulling your storyboard together –

that'll only make it harder for you to deliver your key messages. By investing the time in going through the storyboarding process, you will feel better prepared, which will reward you with increased confidence as you'll have more head space to focus on building rapport with the person you're trying to influence.

KEY TAKEAWAYS
Here's a quick reminder of the steps you can take to help put storytelling theory into practice:

- Harness the power of storytelling to help you make connections and influence other people.
- Use the six storytelling techniques outlined here to bring your influencing story to life.
- Apply Simon Sinek's theory that people buy the 'why', not the 'what'.
- Remember to sell every aspect of your proposition and prove why it will work, using ample facts, insight and visuals.
- Always lead with the benefits, don't just list the features.
- Make it easy for the other party to say 'yes' by taking into account the return on investment and projecting the net benefit.
- Make sure your key messages are concise, with little room for confusion.
- Use the storyboard technique to help create compelling, influential stories.
- Always start with the recommendation (what's it in for them) and work backwards to build your story.
- Think big-picture first, and then dive into the detail.

PART FIVE

DELIVERING AN INFLUENTIAL STORY

No matter how compelling you've made your influential story, if it is not delivered in an inspiring way you'll struggle to convince the other person to say 'yes'. This is the moment of truth – and it's a fact that first impressions really do count! Most people are hard-wired to make snap decisions, so despite all your best laid plans, how you perform live, in the moment, will determine whether you can successfully influence the other party.

Take an interview scenario, for example. Most employers make up their mind about a potential candidate in the first 90 seconds, and then spend the rest of the interview pressure-testing their thinking. Rightly or wrongly, you need to take this into account when delivering a story – as the influencing mantra tells us, 'People buy People'. So, the focus of this Part is how to harness your emotional intelligence to move into the stretch zone and achieve peak performance, whether you're delivering a formal or informal influencing story.

1. HARNESSING YOUR EMOTIONAL INTELLIGENCE TO DELIVER WITH CONFIDENCE

Strong influencers understand that the key to telling an engaging story is to tap into your emotional intelligence and be truly present in the moment. Coaching and professional excellence author Timothy Gallwey highlights this in his book, *The Inner Game of Work*[8] where he argues: Your Performance = Your Potential – Interference.

In other words, reduce the noise in your head (the interference) that prevents you from reaching your full potential, and only then will you be able to perform at your best. This noise is emotional interference – inner fears and concerns that get in the way of performance. Examples could be the need to please, procrastination, stage fright or the fear of failure.

So, in advance of your next influencing opportunity, take the time to self-reflect and ask yourself what are the things that create noise in your head. Then write down how these can be limited, so you can stay focused on the task in hand: delivering your influential story.

Personally, I'm easily distracted by people moving around. And so, to be present in the moment I deliberately position my back to the window whenever possible. This way I'm less likely to be distracted by any commotion taking place on the street outside. I then dial down the interference by opening my notebook and writing the date of the meeting as a way to steady my mind.

EXERCISE

Write down the three main triggers that are likely to distract you in a meeting:

1. ....

2. ....

3. ....

Now make a note of the steps you can take to dial down such noise.

1. ....

2. ....

3. ....

Once your mind is focused, the rest of your emotional intelligence skills can be used to deliver your story with confidence. It will take social skills, self-control, optimism and adaptability to communicate in a confident and credible manner. After all, the other party needs to believe in you and what you're saying if they are to buy into your story. Aim to have a two-way conversation that builds rapport and trust – the last thing it should feel like is a 'pitch' to the other person. Remember to listen with empathy and use self-control to respond, not react, to the conversation. This is often easier said than done, and to make an impact you should manage all aspects of your delivery. Finally, be sure to use optimistic language appropriately, walk the talk and adapt in the moment to ensure that the conversation ebbs and flows naturally.

2. SELLING YOUR INFLUENTIAL STORY WITH IMPACT

As you begin to sell your idea, bear in mind that over time everyone's attention span deteriorates and keeping the other person interested in your story can be a challenge. As such, it's important to think about their frame of mind and take the right steps to keep them engaged and focused on what you have to say. Maintaining the other party's interest levels will depend partly on the content of your story, but as much effort should be put into how you appear, what you say and how you sound. Let's look at each of these in turn:

HOW YOU APPEAR

It may sound obvious, but don't underestimate the importance of thinking about what you're going to wear when you deliver your story. You need to be appropriately turned out – for example, if your meeting is on a Friday, check whether the other party follows an end-of-week *dress down* policy and choose your outfit accordingly.

If you're stepping into an old-school suit and tie culture, take the hint and dress appropriately.

The next step is to learn to walk the talk. Just as it's hard to say something negative with a smile on your face, it's difficult to communicate confidently if your body language suggests that you're a pushover. It's important to be physically approachable and have smiling eyes. By standing tall and making strong eye contact, you will immediately put the other person at ease. If, on the other hand, you look nervous or worried, the likelihood is that they'll mirror this behaviour and start doubting your ability.

Think about where to position yourself in the room. If you are presenting in a formal situation, make sure you sit or stand where you can both read from your slides and maintain confident eye contact with the person you're trying to influence. After all, it's you, not your slides, that will sell your key messages.

Also, ensure that your slide deck supports your words rather than taking attention away from you. The deadliest words in presentation history have to be: *"I know this is too small for you to read, but..."*

You should aim to be authentic and natural, which will make a huge difference in how you come across. Unfortunately, even the most animated individual's personality can disappear when they start a presentation. So, remember not to hand in your personality at reception when you get your visitor's badge! The other party needs to feel that they're getting to know the real you, as this will build trust in the long run.

WHAT YOU SAY

With all the hard work that went into preparing your storyboard, do not go off script and try to wing it. You need to talk with credibility, so resist the temptation to exaggerate or, worse still, make things up to support a point. Your job is to convey to the other party all the information you've prepared and reiterate your key messages. Remember, the other person is hearing your story for the first time and will take a while to get up to speed.

A great way to help you understand how to land your main points is to think about how broadcast newsreaders present information – they start with the headlines, then give you the content and finish with a summary. If you can combine this with passion and enthusiasm, the other person will feel as though they are part of your journey, so constantly re-engage with them throughout your presentation. Try to mirror their body language – this could include nodding when they do or catching their eye and smiling.

You should be building up to the crux of your story – that pivotal moment when you deliver your call to action. At this point, there should be an imaginary drum roll inside your head. Then take your time in spelling out your recommendation; deliver it at a pace that allows the other party to note down what you're asking for. Remember that this should be a summary of what you've already presented – there should be no surprises for either party at this stage, and this should give you confidence.

After you've delivered your recommendation, don't move on too quickly. Instead, take a moment to let them process their thoughts. Above all, choose your words carefully and avoid any 'weak speak' – vague or hackneyed phrases that undermine your credibility.

Below are some common examples of the weak speak and its impact on the other party:

You Say:	They Think:
This potentially could	You are not convinced it will
Hopefully we can agree	You are not sure about it
In all honesty	You are about to exaggerate
With all due respect	You have no respect
To tell you the truth	You are about to lie to me
Believe me, this is a great idea	Even you are not sure about it

Every time you find yourself using one of these phrases, pause and correct yourself by saying, *"What I meant to say was..."* This way you will retrain your brain to use clear and confident language that will help you persuade the other party to agree to your proposition.

HOW YOU SOUND

As a rule, the pace of people's speech speeds up when they're feeling under pressure, so remember to slow yourself down even though you may feel like you're talking at snail's pace. Rather than bombard the other person with information, imagine that you are walking them through your thoughts.

If you want to land a key message, pause to emphasize it. Silence is powerful; it shows that you have something important to say and gives the other party time to think. Avoid rushing your story by getting the right balance between the tone of your voice and the pace of your speech. Fluctuating your tone and volume will help capture the other person's attention. We can all think of an occasion where we zoned out because of a presenter's monotonous voice, so try to keep your tone lively and engaging.

If, despite your best efforts, you notice the other party's attention has started to wander, be quiet and wait until you establish eye contact again before continuing. Then dial up your energy and passion, but resist the temptation to rush.

3. KEEPING THE CONVERSATION FLOWING

A useful analogy to help you understand the importance of building an impactful, influential story is to think about the game of tennis. In tennis, you need to focus as much on preparing for the shot as you do on actually striking the ball and following through. It's the same with an influential story – your role is to make sure your story flows seamlessly so that it's easy to follow. The great news is that there are phrases and closed questions – which can be answered with a single word – you can use to connect the different elements of your story to make it engaging.

It's helpful here to refer back to the STRONG framework for effective phrases that you can use to link together the various aspects of your story.

HOW TO STITCH YOUR STORY TOGETHER

Set the Scene

Open up the conversations and capture the other person's attention by saying, *"I've got an idea I'd like to share with you."*

Tailor the Story

Summarize the needs you've uncovered with your clever questions by saying, *"If I've understood you correctly, your particular challenges are..."* People invariably miss checking off this box, but it's key to helping you confirm whether you're on the right track.

You can then move the conversation on by saying, *"Let me see how I can help"* before going through your story in detail. Remember to sense-check everything with them as you go along by asking, *"Does the detail make sense to you?"*

Recommendation

When you get to this pivotal moment, you need to pause, and then introduce your call to action by saying, *"To be specific"* or *"In summary"* and be sure that you speak slowly and use confident language.

Opportunity

A great way to follow on from your recommendation and show them the size of the prize is to say, *"Let me explain how I arrived at these assumptions."*

Negotiate

The better your influencing story and your ability to deliver it with confidence, the less likely you will end up having to negotiate. So be confident and move straight on to the next steps.

Get to next steps

You are now at the end of your story, so tie everything up by finishing on a positive note and agreeing on when to next get in touch. This could be, *"I'll get the contract over to you"* or *"Let's put a date in the diary for our next meeting."*

By using these closed questions, you'll be able to confirm that the other person is actually listening to you. As discussed, it's important to listen with empathy to uncover the other party's needs, but it's equally important to make sure they are actively listening to your story.

A great way to make sure your story flows well, and is engaging and impactful, is to rehearse your delivery with a colleague or friend. Just like your counterpart in the real business conversation, they won't know what you are about to ask for. Remember to draw on your emotional intelligence to focus on how you appear, what you say and how you sound. Above all, try and keep it simple and make it easy for the other party to say 'yes' by reminding yourself that less is generally more.

KEY TAKEAWAYS

By now you should have a clear understanding of how your emotional intelligence skills can help deliver a compelling, influential story that captures and holds the other individual's attention.

Here's a quick recap:

- First impressions count, so draw on your emotional intelligence to think real-time, in the moment.
- Your Performance = Your Potential − Interference. Reduce the noise in your head so you can focus on the task at hand.
- Be physically approachable and put the other party at ease.
- It should feel like you're having a two-way conversation, not giving a pitch.

- Don't be tempted to go off script – use the content you have prepared, using your storyboard to communicate with confidence.
- Deliver your recommendation at writing pace, using clear and confident language.
- Avoid *weak speak* – those vague or hackneyed phrases that undermine your credibility.
- Use silence to punctuate points, and then re-engage with the other person and give them time to process what you're telling them.
- Fluctuate your pace and tone to keep them interested in what you have to say.
- Create an influential story that engages the other person.
- Practice makes perfect, so rehearse your story with a colleague or friend to confirm that it is compelling and impactful.

PART SIX

CONTROLLING
THE INFLUENTIAL
CONVERSATION

The most challenging aspect of influencing is learning how to control the influencing conversation. No matter how much time you have spent preparing and rehearsing, performing live, in the moment, is easy to envision but hard to do. This is because people are unpredictable, and despite all of our best-laid plans we can't know what noise or interference is going on in the other person's head and how this will impact our conversation. Yet, surprisingly, the majority of sales and influence training on the market focuses on theory and preparation. It gives little attention to the importance of leveraging emotional intelligence to stay in control of the conversation. This Part will give you the tools and techniques to handle interactions effectively and stand out from the competition.

As we've discussed at some length, strong influencers understand that the secret to controlling the conversation is to be truly present in the moment. This means reducing the interference in *your* head – your inner thoughts, worries or concerns – and focusing entirely on the other party. To start with, ensure that the key messages of your offering are clear in your mind and you know exactly how you can help the other party. Self-management in this way will create more headspace, so that instead of relying on prompts or notes you can respond confidently in the moment and interact convincingly.

1. TYPES OF INTERACTIONS IN CONVERSATIONS

First, draw on your self-reliance to identify the different types of interactions that are likely to take place during the influencing conversation. Broadly speaking, there are four types of conversational elements:

1. Questions or statements.
2. Tactics.
3. Issues.
4. Negotiation Points.

Use your ability to think in the moment and to hear, process, judge and categorize the interactions taking place. People often assume that all interactions are geared towards real issues. Unfortunately, not everyone behaves in a principled and above-board manner, so use good judgement and gauge whether the other party is raising genuine concerns or using tactics to shift the balance of power in their favour. Remember, people are different, so refer back to the DISC model in Part Two to help you recognize various communication styles. The more outgoing the person, the more likely you are to spot the different types of interactions in the meeting.

Conversely, the more reserved they are, the less vocal they're likely to be, so you will have to use your emotional intelligence and read their body language to help judge which type of interaction you're facing.

Each of the four interaction types needs to be managed and controlled differently to make it easy for the other person to say 'yes' to your recommendation or request.

2. DEALING WITH QUESTIONS OR STATEMENTS

It's entirely appropriate for the other person to ask questions, in order to better understand what you are asking of them. For example, they may try to establish how your proposal will work, to get a clearer understanding of the timing, or want further explanation about the data you're citing. Respond to these questions as they happen, and don't just close them down. Resist the temptation to say you will only answer questions at the end, as you risk losing their attention. Remember that to be fully engaged you should be listening with empathy the whole time you're sharing your story. It's important to be alert and ready for questions and comments, as there's a high probability that these will precede any of the other interactions (tactics, real issues or negotiation points).

3. TAKING CONTROL OF THEIR TACTICS

The use of tactics can be defined as challenging behaviour designed to weaken and undermine you. An example of this could be someone checking their phone and deliberately avoiding eye contact during the conversation as a way of gaining the upper hand, or a customer trying to get you to lower your price by making an unfair comparison to a competitor. Sometimes people behave in this way deliberately, while at other times it could be unconscious. Regardless of the intention, it's important to recognize tactical conversations and respond appropriately. The following four-step technique can be used to control tactical conversations.

STEP 1 - RECOGNIZE THE TACTIC

A powerful way to recognize the unfair use of tactics is to think about how kids behave when they want to get their own way. This can often involve stamping their feet and asking your other half for something when you've already told them 'no'. Now apply a business lens to this behaviour and think of a time when someone has banged their fists on a table or asked to speak to your boss as a way of shifting the balance of power in their favour.

It's important to consider the other party's DISC profile. Try to anticipate any tactics that may come your way based on the type of personality you're dealing with. If they are an extrovert their tactics are likely to be verbal, whereas if they're more introverted their tactics are likely to be non-verbal and you may need to read their body language to spot their tactics.

STEP 2 - DIAL UP YOUR EMOTIONAL INTELLIGENCE TO RESPOND TO THE TACTIC

Leverage your emotional intelligence and draw on your self-control to *respond* rather than *react* to whatever is being said or done. First, take a deep breath to prepare yourself. Don't feel pressured into reacting – instead, give yourself time to order your thoughts and prepare a response. A great way to balance the playing field is to treat tactics like a game and use humour to diffuse the situation. So, if the other person is belittling your idea by unfavourably comparing it to a competitor's, call them out by saying something like, *"You're comparing apples and pears and they taste rather different!"* It's important to respond with the right tone and keep the mood of the conversation upbeat. After all, your goal is to keep the dialogue flowing, to motivate them on a commercial and emotional level to say 'yes'.

STEP 3 - MOVE THE CONVERSATION ON

You can re-balance things and move the conversation forward by adopting a winning mindset with confident words, tone and body language. Phrases such as, *"We're both here to make money"* or *"Let's agree to move forward like this"* demonstrate that you need to work together to arrive at a mutually successful outcome.

It can be hard to think of how to do this in the moment. So, prepare for any curveballs that may come your way to keep the conversation rolling. Remember, when it comes to controlling tactics, being forewarned really is being forearmed!

STEP 4 - GET BACK TO BUSINESS

Remember that tactics get in the way of true influencing. Once you've spotted the tactic, responded and moved the conversation on, it's time to get back to the business at hand – sharing your compelling, influential story. Take control of the conversation by helping the other party focus. This could involve re-summarizing or agreeing on next steps to keep moving the conversation forward.

Ensure that you follow these four steps in the correct order. Once you've recognized the tactic, you need to call them on it and get back to business as seamlessly as possible, managing the mood throughout the conversation. This means controlling your body language and tone by keeping them situationally appropriate. Remember, if the mood dips you're less likely to achieve closure. By perfecting this process, you will be well on your way to becoming a strong influencer.

4. OVERCOMING REAL ISSUES

It's crucial to use your judgement to determine when the other party is raising a real issue. These are genuine reasons why they may have a problem with some aspect of your proposition. *"We don't have enough budget at the moment"* or *"I can't see how this would work in reality"* could be perfectly legitimate concerns. In many ways, real issues are a positive sign, as they are in effect saying, *"I like your idea, but..."* So, you need to adopt a positive mindset, respect that everyone's entitled to their opinion and embrace any concerns in order to influence them effectively. The following four-step technique can be used to overcome any real issues or concerns with confidence.

STEP 1 - CLARIFY THE ISSUE

In a 'real issue' type of conversation you need to find a solution to change the other person's mind. The first step to achieving this is to demonstrate that you're actively listening by asking questions that will clarify what the person's really concerned about. An example could be, *"What is it about the timing that's worrying you?"* By asking questions like this, you show that you value the other individual's opinion, and they will appreciate being listened to. In fact, they might even talk themselves out of the issue. Your role is to facilitate the process – after all, a problem shared is a problem halved. The more information you can gather about their issue or concern, the more likely you are to be able to find a solution.

STEP 2 - PUT EVERY ISSUE ON THE TABLE

Once you have addressed the first issue, the smart thing to do is to ask if there's anything else you can help them with. Take the time to ask, *"Is there something else that's bothering you?"* or *"If that wasn't an issue, would you go ahead?"* By helping them put all of their concerns on the table you'll encourage them to process your call to action, then and there, and facilitate a smoother, more efficient path to closure. Taking notes on their issues and concerns demonstrates that you are listening and will help you later when you're ready to deal with their concerns.

STEP 3 - PRIORITIZE THE ISSUES

Now that you have clarified all the issues, you need to try and get them to share with you their needs and desires in order of importance. Start by dealing with their biggest issue first. Ask them outright, *"Of these issues, which is the biggest hurdle stopping you from saying you can go ahead?"* This question will prevent you from assuming that you know their main problem when this may not be the case. Resist the temptation to repeat or read out the list of issues you've captured, since this may dredge up smaller, less significant concerns.

STEP 4 - CHANGE THEIR MIND

You should now be in a strong position to deal with the other person's real issues and help them change their mind. There are different ways to achieve this without having to fundamentally change your call to action. You could highlight a specific data point or potential benefit to convince them to say 'yes'. For example, if their concern is that your idea will cost too much in the short term, you could show how they'll recoup their investment over time, or that the payback will in fact surpass their original outlay.

Be creative with the solutions you suggest. If, despite your best efforts, you really can't change their mind, you should go into negotiation mode and find an overlapping position. But remember, you should never agree to a deal that provides you with little or no return. That's tantamount to walking away empty-handed, despite all the time and effort you put into the influencing conversation. If you need to invest additional resources, always ask for something in return.

Don't worry if you can't always provide a solution on the spot – you may need to say that you'll have to get back to them. Whenever possible, though, try to anticipate and identify potential challenges as part of your preparation. Fill in the table opposite to help get around roadblocks and rework your proposition.

EXERCISE: ANTICIPATE THEIR REAL ISSUE

WHAT WILL THEY SAY THEIR ISSUES ARE?	BEST WAY TO CHANGE THEIR MIND

Every time you go into an influencing conversation, retrain your brain to think through likely issues or curveballs. Plan for the interaction types and the solutions that will change the other party's mind. During the conversation keep your wits about you and constantly analyse what is being discussed to determine if it is a question, an issue, a tactic or a negotiation point.

A great way to improve your ability to assess the type of interaction and articulate the best response is to adopt the principle of *plan, do and review*. Keep a record of the actual interactions versus what you had planned, and reflect on how your responses impacted the conversation and your ability to stay in control. You may not get it right every time, but to once again quote Zig Ziglar, *"You don't have to be great to start, but you have to start to be great."*

It's important to deal with real issues at the right time in your story in order to stay in control of the influential conversation. Remember my definition of a 'real issue' – it's a concern they have with your recommendation. Again, use the STRONG framework in Part Four to understand **when** to deal with them.

5. CLOSING WITH CONFIDENCE

The final stage in controlling the influential conversation is to close with confidence. As the saying goes, strong influencers should 'always be closing'. This means harnessing your ambition and being on the front foot so that you can agree on next steps. You should assume that the other party will say 'yes' to your recommendation because you will have already answered their questions, taken control of their tactics and provided solutions for their real issues. A rookie mistake is to finish your story and wait for the other person to respond. A strong influencer will always put the next steps on the table as a way of flushing out whether the other party is on board or not. A good example of how to close confidently is to say, *"I will see HR to get the paperwork signed"* or *"Let's get the next meeting in the diary."* Resist the temptation to use fear as a way of closing, by saying something like, *"If you don't say yes today, I'm going to have to share this idea with someone else."* This approach is likely to undo any rapport and trust you've developed. Similarly, avoid using email to close, as it gives the other party extra thinking time that could lead to more concerns. Instead, be specific and outline simple, definitive next steps. If at this stage they don't agree to your recommendation, you may have to negotiate.

6. INFLUENCING VIA PHONE AND EMAIL

Unfortunately, technology has made it increasingly tempting for people to avoid face-to-face interactions. The fact remains that when it comes to influencing, meeting in person really makes a difference. It sends a clear message that you think the meeting is important, it's a good way to build a relationship and you'll be more likely to achieve closure. On a phone call, for example, you will hear the other person's words and tone of voice, but you won't be able to read their body language and are therefore less likely to uncover their real needs. Email is even tougher – you only have the words to rely on and, as noted in Part Three, words alone account for just 7% of interpersonal communication. The good news is that since fewer people are taking the initiative to meet in person, you have the opportunity to differentiate yourself by going the extra mile with an in-person conversation.

If it's just not possible to meet face-to-face, perhaps because of geographical or time constraints, at a minimum use Skype or pick up the phone. Email really should be your last resort, so try to resist requests to send your presentation electronically in place of hosting an actual meeting. As mentioned, it's you not your slides that influence the other party. Remind yourself of how many emails get deleted without a second glance and take positive steps to avoid having yours become spam.

Finally, be resilient. It takes tenacity and perseverance to influence others, so always follow up with the other party and maintain control throughout all your interactions. Remember, your recommendation won't be as high on their agenda as they will be on yours, so make sure you keep nudging them. Yet, don't bombard them with calls – your aim is to influence them, not irritate them!

KEY TAKEAWAYS

You should now have the self-awareness to recognize the four different types of interactions – and possess the self-control – to *respond* rather than *react* to each of them. Here's a quick summary to help you control the influencing conversation:

- Be truly present in the moment in order to control the dialogue.
- Make sure you know your story inside-out so you can focus on handling the interaction with the other party.
- Use your judgement to categorize and process the four different types of interaction: Questions, Tactics, Real Issues and Negotiation Points.
- Respond to questions and statements as they come up, but recognize that they may embody a tactic, real issue or negotiation point.
- Use your emotional intelligence to recognize when the other party is using unfair tactics to shift the balance of power in their favour.
- Follow four steps to take control of their tactics: recognize the tactic; respond rather than react to it; move the conversation forward; get back to the business at hand.

- Learn to differentiate between a tactic and a real issue when it comes to the other person saying 'no' to your recommendation.
- Once you've uncovered a real issue, you need to clarify it and note any other issues, prioritize them so you can focus on the most important ones, and find a solution that helps change the other person's mind.
- If you can't find a solution, you need to start negotiating in order to find an overlapping position. But, remember never to concede if it leaves you with no return.
- As part of your preparation, try to anticipate any tactics or curveballs that may come your way.
- Only respond to real issues once you've fully articulated your story, or you risk losing control of the conversation.
- Always close your influential story with confidence by agreeing on next steps.
- Whenever possible, try to influence in person rather than by phone or email.
- Strong influencers are resilient – follow up to make sure your proposal stays front-and-centre on the other party's agenda.

PART SEVEN

KEEPING FIT FOR INFLUENCING

Congratulations on reaching the final Part of *The Influence Book*. You now have the tools and techniques necessary to be a strong influencer. At this point you should be positioned to:

- Have a clear understanding of how to use your emotional intelligence to develop a confident mindset.
- Prepare for influencing success.
- Build a balanced relationship with the other party.
- Create and deliver a compelling, influencing story.
- Manage and control the influencing conversation.

Of course, it would be wonderful if just by reading this book you could become a certified *strong influencer*. But unfortunately, to really hone your commercial skills takes practice. A powerful analogy to illustrate this point comes from the world of sport. It takes ambition, dedication and hard work to become a world-class athlete, and these attributes are just as important in the business world. **So, to get the most out of this book and become a strong influencer, use it as a workbook**. Underline key points, make notes in the margins and re-do the exercises to help embed your learning.

Using the step-by-step approach provided in Part One, you will have progressed from unconscious competence (you don't realize what you don't know), to conscious incompetence (you know what you need to learn), to conscious competence (you're trying to apply your newly developed influencing skills).

The final and most challenging step on your journey is the move to unconscious competence, where influencing becomes second nature. This takes an enormous amount of effort and commitment, so try to use every opportunity available to practise and hone your influencing skills.

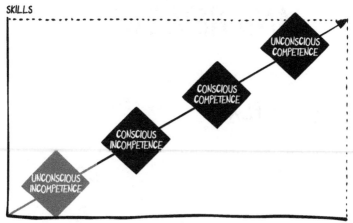

SKILLS

UNCONSCIOUS COMPETENCE

CONSCIOUS COMPETENCE

CONSCIOUS INCOMPETENCE

UNCONSCIOUS INCOMPETENCE

TRAINING

1. ADOPTING THE PRINCIPLE OF *PLAN, DO* AND *REVIEW*

PLAN

DO

REVIEW

The principle of *plan, do and review* can be a useful tool to take your influencing skills to the next level. There will be certain influencing skills that you instinctively summon up and others that you'll find more challenging. A great way to supercharge your learning is to focus on the most difficult areas. So, plan ahead and set yourself a specific influencing goal. An example could be, *"Use the STRONG storyboard framework to create and deliver a compelling, influencing story."* You can also build your story and deliver it during a meeting or in a less formal influencing conversation.

Finally, review the conversation and determine how it went. Ask yourself what worked well and what could have been improved upon. Did your story flow naturally or was it stilted? Was it compelling or did you lose the other person's attention? Don't be tempted to just focus on whether or not you achieved the outcome you'd wanted. It's not just about what you achieved – it's also about how you changed the other person's behaviour.

Remember to rehearse, do a dry run with colleagues or friends and ask for their frank feedback in the lead-up to the actual influencing conversation. If you're feeling brave, ask them to film you as you practice articulating your story – this will help you gauge how confidently you come across in your body language, tone of voice and overall presentation. Remind yourself that feedback is a gift. By adopting this approach, you'll find that over time you move from being consciously competent to unconsciously competent in your engagement.

2. RAISING THE BAR

As discussed in the introduction, strong influencers have a growth mindset and are constantly looking for ways to raise the bar. To continue to develop your skills, use the table below to set influencing goals, identify relevant situations or opportunities and find the necessary support to help you achieve your objectives. See it as your own personalized training plan – a regimen that will help you get fit for influencing success.

MY INFLUENCING COMMITMENT	WHEN What specific meeting/ influencing opportunity?	MY PERSONAL TRAINER Who needs to be involved? Who will hold me to account?

Once you've identified the key influencing skills that you want to improve, ask yourself the following four questions before each and every situation. The answers will help you pull together all the influencing elements, up your game and achieve the desired outcome.

4 STRONG QUESTIONS

1. How will I build the relationship and flex my style?

To answer this, refer back to Maslow's triangle of needs to understand the other party's requirements and build a relationship with them. Use the DISC tool to identify your and your counterpart's communication styles, to understand the best way to get in sync.

2. What is my recommendation and compelling story?

For the answer to this question use the STRONG storyboard framework to structure your influencing story. Remember to start with end in mind, work out what's in it for them, and then work backwards from there.

3. How will I stay in control and handle their interactions?

Draw on your self-control to manage the influencing situation real-time, in the moment. Use the control techniques outlined in Part Six to help you maintain composure as you help them overcome doubts or change their mind about any issues or concerns they may have.

4. How will I deliver a strong performance?

Remember to avoid *weak speak* and use clear, confident language. It's important to walk the talk and fluctuate your tone and pitch to keep the other person fully engaged in what you have to say.

By taking the time to answer each of these four questions in turn, you'll reap the rewards of increased confidence and improved performance.

3. NETWORKING FOR SUCCESS

Networking provides the ideal opportunity to put your newly acquired influencing skills to the test. Now, if the mere mention of the word 'networking' has you breaking out in a cold sweat, you're certainly not alone. Many people would rather be strapped into the dentist's chair than attend a networking event with a room full of strangers. However, in today's relentlessly competitive world, the ability to make new connections lies at the heart of business success.

With this in mind, I wanted to finish this book by sharing some of my top tips on how to network successfully so you can use every available opportunity to build your personal brand and become even more influential.

Generally speaking, there are three types of people: takers, matchers and givers. A taker will always position themselves at the centre of the agenda; a matcher will adopt a 'you scratch my back and I'll scratch yours' approach; a giver will be prepared to go the extra mile on behalf of the other party. Strong influencers tend to be givers. It's not necessary to please all of the people all of the time – instead, you should aim to be generous to others more often than not.

In general, if you love your network, your network will love you. So, always respond promptly to requests, as it's unprofessional – and downright impolite – to ignore emails or phone messages. By drawing on your emotional intelligence and putting yourself in the other person's shoes, you'll build credibility and trust that will pay big dividends. After all, what goes around comes around. If you say you'll follow up with a new contact, make sure that you actually do. This could involve connecting with them via social media or arranging to meet face-to-face.

Your aim should be to seek out every opportunity to grow your network. This could include attending conferences, socializing with colleagues at the pub after work or contributing to industry-specific forums online.

Start by listing the people with whom you have a good relationship and who can help you achieve your goals. These people should be your primary focus. Then make a list of those you don't yet have a relationship with, but who can help you reach your goals. This list of contacts should be your secondary focus. Finally, put the people who are not on your radar, and aren't necessarily important to you right now, onto your third list of priorities.

Having identified a list of 'primary focus' people in your network, you should now prioritize building relationships with them so that you can successfully influence them. This can be achieved by following the five principles overleaf:

1. **Be interested:** Ask 'clever' questions to understand their particular challenges, and make sure you listen carefully to their response.
2. **Be interesting:** You need to have something to say, so prepare your elevator pitch ahead of time to help capture their attention and get your message across clearly and succinctly. Your aim is to differentiate yourself from competitors, clearing maximum airspace.
3. **Be generous:** Be prepared to invest your time with the other person – you don't have to give something away for free but be appropriately giving.
4. **Make connections:** Find the overlap that you both want. It could be a pertinent article that you think may be of interest to them, which gives either one of you reason to pick up the phone and call.
5. **Keep in touch:** Don't just take their business card and leave it at that – make sure to follow up on your conversation and start building a relationship. But don't bombard them with emails; your aim is to show how you can help, not to be a pest!

By nurturing your relationships in these ways, and behaving in an authentic, generous manner, you will be well on your way to winning other people's hearts and minds and being perceived as an influential person. Strong influencers understand that legacy really does matter.

With this in mind, I will leave you with the words of one of history's most influential storytellers.

"People will forget what you said, people will forget what you did, but people will never forget how you made them feel."

Maya Angelou

KEY TAKEAWAYS

As you continue on your journey to becoming a strong influencer, here's a final reminder of the steps you can take to keep fit for influencing success:

- Seek out new opportunities to put the influencing theory into practice. Remember, it takes ambition and hard work to raise your influencing game.
- Identify specific influencing goals, and then adopt the principle of *plan, do and review*.
- Ask for feedback from colleagues and friends, and then have the courage to act on it.
- Complete your personalized training program by identifying your goal, the relevant opportunity and who can help you achieve it.
- Ask yourself the four STRONG questions before every influencing situation to boost your confidence and improve your performance.
- Put your influencing skills to the test by pursuing relevant networking opportunities.
- Become a 'giver' and be appropriately generous to others.
- Prioritize the people you already have a relationship with who can help you achieve your goals.
- Keep in touch. Remember to follow up with new contacts and stay connected with them, in person or via social media.

FURTHER READING

- *A Theory of Human Motivation*, Abraham Maslow, 1943
- *Drive: The Surprising Truth About What Motivates Us*, Daniel Pink, 2011
- *Eat That Frog – 21 Great Ways To Stop Procrastinating And Get More Done In Less Time*, Brian Tracy, 2007
- *Emotional Capitalists: The Ultimate Guide For Developing Emotional Intelligence For Leaders*, Dr Marytn Newman, 2014
- *Emotional Intelligence: Why It Can Matter More Than IQ*, Dan Goleman, 1996
- *Getting To Yes: Negotiating An Agreement Without Giving In*, Roger Fish & William Ury, 2012
- *How To Win Friends And Influence People*, Dale Carnegie, 1936
- *In Business As In Life, You Don't Get What You Deserve, You Get What You Negotiate*, Chester L. Karrass, 1999
- *Mindset – The New Psychology of Success,* Carol Dweck, 2006
- *7 Habits Of Highly Effective People*, Stephen Covey, 2004
- *Start With The Why: How Great Leaders Inspire Everyone To Take Action*, Simon Sinek, 2011
- *Silent Messages: Implicit Communication of Emotions and Attitude*, Albert Mehrabian, 1971
- *The Effective Executive*, Peter Drucker, 2007
- *The Chimp Paradox*, Steve Peters, 2012
- *The Inner Game of Work*, Tim Gallwey, 2000
- *The Mindfulness Book: Practical Ways To Lead A More Mindful Life*, Dr Martyn Newman, 2016
- *The Negotiation Book: Practical Steps to Becoming a Master Negotiator*, Nicole Soames, 2017

- *The Psychology of Selling*, Brian Tracy, 1995
- *Time To Think – Listening To Ignite The Human Mind*, Nancy Kline, 2002
- *To Sell Is Human,* Daniel Pink, 2014
- *Who Moved My Cheese?*, Spencer Johnson, 1999
- *Women Don't Ask*, Linda Babcock & Sara Laschever, 2007
- *Working With Emotional Intelligence*, Dan Goleman, 1998

REFERENCES

1   Dweck, C. (2007), *Mindset: The New Psychology of Success*, Random House, New York.

2   Newman, M. (2014), *Emotional Capitalists: The Ultimate Guide For Developing Emotional Intelligence For Leaders*, RocheMartin, London.

3   Maslow, A. (1943), *A Theory of Human Motivation*, Psychological Review.

4   Mehrabian, A. (1971), *Silent Messages: Implicit Communication of Emotions and Attitude*, Wadsworth Publishing Company, Belmont, CA.

5   Bower, G. & Clark, M. (1969), *Narrative Stories as Mediators for Serial Learning*, Springer-Verlag, Norwell, MA.

6   Sinek, S. (2009), *How Great Leaders Inspire Action*, TEDx Talk, www.ted.com/talks.

7   Soames, N. (2017), *The Negotiation Book: Practical Steps to Becoming a Master Negotiator*, LID Publishing, London.

8   Gallwey, T. (2000), *The Inner Game of Work*, Random House, New York.

ACKNOWLEDGMENTS

I couldn't finish writing a book on influencing without thanking the two people who have been such important role models in my life. They are my mother, for always challenging the status quo and inspiring me to constantly push myself into my stretch zone, and my father, for showing me how far-reaching my sphere of influence can be, and who is himself living testimony that you really can teach an old dog new tricks!

I'd like to thank Dr Martyn Newman, who was truly influential in my professional life by introducing me to the power of emotional intelligence. This has enabled me to develop commercial training and coaching programs interwoven with emotional intelligence principles that deliver real impact in the business world. My motivation for writing this book was to share my passion for helping people harness their emotional intelligence so they can be their very best with an even wider audience.

Thanks to my fantastic family – my husband James and my daughters Talya and Amelie – who help me put my influencing skills to the test on a daily basis!

Also deserving special mention is my wonderful team at Diadem, for their energy, enthusiasm and commitment, and Katharine Wijsman in particular for being a great sounding board as I wrote this book.

Finally, thanks to Martin Liu, Niki Mullin and Sara Taheri at LID Publishing for their encouragement, expertise and support – it was a pleasure to work with them for a second time. Here's to working together on book number three!

ABOUT THE AUTHOR

NICOLE SOAMES is a highly qualified coach and emotional intelligence practitioner. She gained extensive commercial experience during 12 years of managing large sales teams at Unilever and United Biscuits, followed by 15 years developing and delivering training programmes around the globe. In 2009 Nicole founded Diadem, a leading commercial skills training and coaching company. With 85 clients in 12 countries, Diadem has helped thousands of people become *commercial athletes* in influencing and selling, negotiation, account management, marketing, presenting, strategy, coaching, leadership and management. Nicole is also the best-selling author of *The Negotiation Book*, part of the Concise Advice Series from LID Publishing.

Follow Nicole on Twitter **@diademperform**
Or visit the website **www.diademperformance.com**

BY THE SAME AUTHOR

ISBN: 978-1-911687-85-6

ISBN: 978-1-912555-53-6

ISBN: 978-1-911498-42-1

ISBN: 978-1-912555-71-0